Titles in this series

Voices and Images of Nunavimmiut

Volume 8: Economic Development

Part II:
Business & Investment,
Housing & Construction,
Careers & Training

Volume 8:
Economic Development

Part II
Business & Investment, Housing & Construction,
Careers & Training

Voices and Images of Nunavimmiut

Volume editors:
Minnie Grey, Peter Mittenthal & Marianne Stenbaek

IPI Press

Distributed by McGill-Queens University Press

Published in Collaboration with

McGill Institute for the Study of Canada
L'Institut d'études canadiennes de McGill

Will Straw, Director.

First Edition copyright © 2014 IPI Press

Maps used by permission of Nunavik Research
Centre, Makivik Corporation

Design: IPI Press
Cover illustration: Sammy Kudluk
Series editors: Minnie Grey & Marianne Stenbaek

ISBN 978-0-9829155-8-5

Printed in Canada

IPI
Press

Post Office Box 212
Hanover, New Hampshire 03755 USA

*Attributions for article authors and illustrators
are listed when known.*

Contents

Introduction

When first asked to write this, I wondered what I could focus on to best describe economic development especially in Nunavik. On a quick note, I am not an academic and this is not an economic dissertation, but I do have about 47 years experience in different elements of the economy.

I was not asked to explain "economic development," however I think it is important to remember what is meant by the term. "Economic development is the sustained, concerted actions of policy makers and communities that promote the standard of living and economic health of a specific area." You will find this definition all over the web, whether it is Wikipedia, the World Bank or other agencies.

Economic development is led by those that have a view of how they can make a profit for the benefit of the owner and the community at large. Some of the larger groups involved in Nunavik are Makivik Corporation and Federation Cooperatives, Nouveau Québec (FCNQ).

There are various sectors that are contributing factors to our Nunavik economy. The retail sector has both the FCNQ and also the Northwest Company as the largest contributors to this sector, however there are many other less visible elements that are essential contributors. These are the local small stores that are owned and operated in the main part by local people in each community. The new economy appearing on a screen somewhere in someone's house are the sell/swap sites in each community throughout the north. However while these are retail in one form or another they are essentially providing a local outlet for many producers but in particular the "Arts and Crafts" manufacturers. The woman sewing at home–a Parka, Kamiks, mitts, earrings, bracelets, and many other items–but also teaching others their skills. These retail sales are important to the economy; they provide employment and income for many throughout Nunavik.

Government institutes play an ever-increasing role in the economy, as they are a large employer in the region and throughout the north. Government's have expanding roles in economic development through the north. However government is not a wealth creator, this is usually left with the private sector. Government through its various economic development programs continue to play a role but often delivery, timing and criteria make these programs difficult, however efforts by both Makivik Corporation and Kativik Regional Development have made the one stop shopping process for entrepreneurs a success story.

Tourism has been an economic driver for over 5 decades in Nunavik; due to world economic circumstances the consumptive tourism of hunting and fishing outfitting is in decline. This is also due to competition from many other remote locations that are of interest to those that have the financial capacity. Through the establishment of provincial and national parks and the supporting infrastructure there has been significant investment and as a result increased interest and development of adventure and non-consumptive tourism.

The extraction economy in Nunavik consists of shrimp fishing and mining. The mining industry in Nunavik has had a long history of development with Asbestos mine at "Asbestos

Hill" being the first to have actually produced materials for export through the 70s and in to the eighties. This has since been followed by two nickel mines in the same area. The first asbestos mine returned very little economic benefit to the local people. The advent of the James Bay Northern Québec Agreement and subsequent Impact and Benefit Agreements, changed the landscape. Mining companies are now obligated to carry out many environmental remediation processes but of greater significance is the impact on the local and regional economies of not only revenue sharing but he awarding of various contracts to beneficiary owned companies and the employment.

Fishing has been around for a long time and has been able to sustain the Inuit for centuries. Commercial efforts were carried out by the Moravian mission and also by the Hudson's Bay Company with limited success. Other commercial efforts have been through the cooperatives. The northern shrimp fishery has been a part of the Nunavik economy for thirty-six years starting with research and moving into commercial operations within a couple of years. Our efforts first started in Ungava Bay and Hudson Strait and into Davis Strait from 1979 to 1984 and then into the Labrador Sea. From the start of this fishery we have sold the shrimp on world markets and in the early years to Scandinavia, Europe and Japan. Today these same shrimp are sold into China, Russia and the European Union and Scandinavia. These are very competitive markets with competition from southern based companies and producers in Greenland and to a lesser extent Norway and Iceland.

The economic viability of the fishery is closely tied to the health of the shrimp stocks from Newfoundland to the Davis Strait. A great deal of time and effort is placed on ensuring that we maintain the shrimp biomass in a healthy condition. Compliance requirement to meet the scientific requirements of the regulatory agencies is very comprehensive. Issues of by-catch of other fish have been addressed for twenty years and little or no by-catch occurs in this fishery.

The market is the determining factor in how much we make from year to year. Profit margins can be very narrow and over the years there has been consolidation in the industry, this has been done in order to enhance the viability of the fishing effort and increase the value of the license. The industry is not without its ups and downs, most of which again is determined by the consumer. We are selling a natural product from a very pristine area, which has some natural environmental conditions called ice to protect the stock for a large part of the year. The Inuit of Nunavik and members of the offshore shrimp industry can be proud of their achievements in discovering and managing this fishery for the future of all concerned.

Neil Greig

Neil Greig has been involved in fisheries, economic development and management for the last 45 years.

ᐃᕗᔨᕕᒃ
Ivujivik
ᓴᓪᓗᐃᑦ
Salluit
ᐊᑯᓕᕕᒃ
Akulivik
ᐳᕕᕐᓂᑐᖅ
Puvirnituq
ᑕᓯᐅᔭᕐᔪᐊᖅ
ᐃᓄᒃᔪᐊᒃ
Inukjuak
Hudson
Bay
ᓴᓂᑭᓗᐊᒃ
Sanikiluaq
ᐅᒥᐅᔭᒃ
Umiujaq
ᑰᒡᔪᐊᕌᐱᒃ
Kuujjuarapik
55
N
U

ᓴᓪᓗᐃᒃ

son Strait

ᐃᕐᓯᐊᖅ
giqsujuaq

ᖁᐊᖅᑕᖅ
Quaqtaq

ᐅᖓᕙ
Ungava
Bay

k

ᑲᖏᖅᓱᐊᓗᔾᔪᐊᖅ
Kangiqsualujjuaq

ᑯᑦᔪᐊᖅ
uujjuaq

L

A V I K

People Discuss Their Corporation: Makivik Tours Northern Québec
By Willie Adams

In an information and fact finding tour, the President
of the Makivik Corporation, Charlie Watt, explained to
the people of the various communities the financial status
of a number of companies that have been established by
Makivik. He also outlined the constitution and offshore
island issues that will soon have to be negotiated. The response Mr. Watt received was that almost all the communities were in favour of Makivik's activities in establishing companies and most indicated that they were ready to
participate in the economic development of the territory
by having Makivik companies set up in their communities.
In addition, Mr. Watt got a great deal of support for his efforts to negotiate control for the Inuit of the offshore area,
especially before these islands are given over to Québec by
the federal government. Furthermore, all the communities
that Mr. Watt visited, including Povungnituk and Ivujivik,
supported the idea that Inuit should take action to become
involved in the rewriting of the Canadian constitution.

Also accompanying Mr. Watt on the trip to the seven
communities of the Hudson Coast and the Hudson Strait
was the First Vice-President of Makivik, Kakinik Naluiyuk,
and Jobie Epoo, a director. They travelled with a secretary,
photographer, and reporters from IGALAAO and *Atuaqnik*
newspapers. Unfortunately, the trip was cut short after a

week because of an emergency meeting that suddenly came up in Montréal concerning the possible purchase of Nordair, that needed the personal attention of Charlie Watt. However, he plans to complete his trip to the communities along the Ungava Coast as soon as possible.

Generally, all the meetings were very well attended, except in Povungnituk, where Makivik officials met only the Community Council there. Apparently, as explained by the President of the Povungnituk Council, there must be at least a one week notice before a public meeting can be held in Povungnituk.

One of the main purposes of the tour was to inform the people about the development and financial status of the companies that have been established by the Makivik Corporation. To date these companies include Air Inuit, Inuit Leasing, Ayapiqvik Restaurant, Imaqpik Fisheries, and Kigiak Builders Inc.

Air Inuit

Right from the beginning of the trip to Great Whale River the question of having Air Inuit operate on the Hudson Coast was brought up. In Great Whale the people asked if this was possible and one person said that even the Crées wanted to know if one of Air Inuit's planes could operate out of that community on a contract basis. In Akulivik the people indicated that it would be a good idea if Air Inuit could provide a good service along the Hudson Coast and explained that at the moment, there are problems in traveling to the Ungava Coast for such things as meetings because there are no direct flights connecting the two coasts. People in Inukjuak pointed out that airline services would improve if there were larger planes flying routes.

Charlie Watt answered that at the moment, for the purpose of airline service, Northern Quebec is split into two, with Air Inuit operating on one side and Austin Airways operating on the other side. But if the people of Great Whale supported it, Air Inuit could always apply for a license to operate along the Hudson Coast. In Inukjuak, Mr. Watt explained to the people that Air Inuit was now operating a larger aircraft which is called the "Caribou." However, he said there were still some problems with it because most of the airstrips in the communities are not wide enough for it right now.

Although the people indicated that Austin Airways provides a fairly good service, generally the people put forth the idea that Air Inuit should operate in the Hudson Coast too and that many would give their support on this.

Inuit Leasing

For the most part, the people did not have too many questions about Inuit Leasing. In Great Whale someone asked where Inuit Leasing airplanes were used, and in Inukjuak another person wanted to know if that company leases other things besides planes. Charlie Watt answered that the aircraft brought by this company were mainly leased for long periods of time to large corporations in the south or to government agencies. He also explained that

Inuit Leasing can buy, sell, and lease airplanes, and that it does not necessarily have to deal only in airplanes

Imaqpik Fisheries

Concerning Imaqpik Fisheries, Mr. Watt generally informed the people of the different communities that their operation with a ship in the Davis Strait was proceeding very well. The Inuit who were working there were satisfied with the conditions. He stated that there will be more Inuit working in that area next year and that Imaqpik might have more than two ships then. However, there were problems with Imaqpik's fishing and research operation in the Ungava Bay. The Inuit did not get along well with the crew of the ship. Apparently they could not understand each other with non-English speaking crew and the food that was served also was a cause of problems. Charlie Watt explained that Imaqpik learned from what had happened with the Ungava Bay operation and in the future, they will look into all factors before leasing a ship for the fisheries.

In Inukjuak a person asked if Imaqpik was having trouble selling the shrimp that was being caught. Mr. Watt replied by saying that the market for selling shrimp in Europe is very good at the moment, and that later, when Imaqpik grows larger, they will find buyers in countries such as Japan. In Akulivik, the President of Makivik clarified a misunderstanding about how the Inuit who worked for Imaqpik Fisheries are to be paid. Mr. Watt explained that people will get about half their pay right after they have worked, and once the shrimp is sold, they will receive the rest of their share of the money made on the sale of shrimp. Also stated was that the minimum age for getting a job with the fisheries is 15 years old and that anyone interested should give their names to the Imaqpik office in Kuujjuaq.

Kigiak Builders

A lot of people were interested in finding out more about Kigiak builders. In Great Whale they asked about possible jobs and training with Kigiak, including whether or not it is necessary to be able to speak English to get such jobs with the construction company. Mr. Watt answered that anyone could approach Kigiak if they want to work for the company. He also explained that people could choose the type of work they would like to receive training in, such as electrical, carpentry, plumbing or mechanics. In Akulivik it was explained that there are 21 Inuit working for Kigiak.

Generally, Charlie Watt described the equipment Kigiak now has and how it will operate. He said that it had a cement factory and a large rock crusher. At the moment the rock crusher is being used to build up a five year supply of crushed rock for Chimo and then it will be transported to the other settlements to ensure that all communities will get enough gravel.

In Inukjuak the people who attended the meeting suggested that it would be an improvement if it would be possible for Kigiak to take over MTPA.

Ayapiqvik Restaurant

Ayapiqvik Restaurant sparked a lot of interest in most of the communities that the Makivik officials visited. For example, the people of Great Whale wanted to open a similar type of restaurant in their community. They also indicated that an establishment of a hotel would be a good idea since a lot of people pass through their community when traveling either up the coast or down south. In Inukjuak it was felt that Ayapiqvik could expand their operations by having other communities open up restaurants too. They also thought that it would be wise to conduct the proper research and studies for the communities that decide to open such an operation. Also pointed out was that proper hotels would help with patients that have to travel because current arrangements are not too good. In addition, the people of Akulivik make it known that they too would like to establish a restaurant operation in their community.

To these requests, Charlie Watt explained that any community that wanted to establish something should first plan how they want to set it up and submit a proposal to their Kuujjuaq office.

Offshore Negotiations

During the trip Charlie Watt informed the communities about the situation concerning the offshore area. Inuit claims to this area have never been settled and it was not included in the James Bay and Northern Québec Agreement. Yet, as Mr. Watt described to the people, the federal government is thinking about handing over the offshore area to Québec. He said that a similar type of situation was going to happen with the offshore area around Newfoundland. He said that the Inuit should be fully involved with whatever happens with the islands and the offshore area, and that Ottawa should first negotiate with the Inuit of Northern Québec before the status of the islands for the offshore area is changed or given over to Québec.

The people reacted by stating that the islands have long been used by the Inuit and just about all the communities fully supported Makivik in trying to protect Inuit rights to the offshore area. Only Povungnituk did not give an immediate answer. Other communities such as Akulivik and Ivujivik said they really use the islands for hunting purposes and that action should be taken before any of this area is handed over to Québec.

The Constitution

Charlie Watt also took advantage of his tour to provide a greater explanation of the constitutional issue. He informed the people that in the past the Inuit were never involved in writing or amending the constitution. Mr. Watt said this is why the Inuit can not change a number of things which they are not satisfied with.

The response of the people was very positive with many people understanding the importance of the issue. All the communities were in favour of action, but Povungnituk wanted to find out exactly what is in the constitution before going any further with a position. Nevertheless, Charlie Watt told them that the constitution issue would prob-

ably be the last chance to change things that both ITN and Makivik did not like. In Ivujivik the people seemed happy about the fact that a joint committee was set up by ITC so that Inuit of Labrador, Northern Québec, and NWT could combine to put pressure for changes in the constitution. Another person from Ivujivik also suggested that perhaps it would be better if ITN and Makivik worked together on the constitutional issue.

Relocating to Richmond Gulf

During the meeting in Great Whale River, the question of moving to Richmond Gulf was discussed for awhile. The Makivik officials reported that the relocation to Richmond Gulf would cost between $29 and $32 million, while improving Great Whale would cost about $15 million. They also said that there will be an election on the matter sometime next March or April to determine how many people want to relocate. If the majority wants to move, then relocation to Richmond Gulf could proceed, but there would still be a need to conduct move studies on the matter. However, if the majority want to stay, then the solution will be to improve the community.

It should be noted that the Great Whale people expressed a strong interest in setting up a restaurant and hotel operation in their community because they feel that it is a good position for such a business. In fact, Charlie Tooktoo and Alec Takatuk, both employees for Makivik, were appointed to look into the matter and give their results to the Makivik Corporation.

Makivik Recognizes the People of Povungnituk

Makivik's meeting in Povungnituk was not the same as the other communities because they only met with the directors of the Community Council, although a few people came in to listen. They mainly talked about the offshore negotiations and the constitution. However, the question of Makivik's resolution not to recognize ITN anymore was brought up. To this, Mr. Watt explained that the resolution in question was directed only towards the ITN organization and that Makivik will still recognize and deal with the population of Povungnituk and Ivujivik.

A Quick Meeting in Salluit

In Salluit (Sugluk) only the constitution and the offshore islands were discussed because Charlie Watt was already rushed to get to Montréal for the emergency meeting about Nordair. The other topics that were usually discussed in the meetings were heard over the local FM radio station from tapes that Kakinik Naluiyuk had recorded. Generally, the people offered a lot of support for Makivik 's negotiations on the offshore question, and the constitutional issue.

A Different Sort of Meeting in Wakeham Bay

The meeting in Wakeham Bay was different from the others. The President of the Community Council invited the President of ITN, Quppaq Tayara, to the meeting and it turned into more of a debate between ITN and Makivik.

The main question that was asked was what are the

goals of ITN and Makivik. The people were also concerned about the extinguishment of rights by the federal government's Bill C-9. Charlie Watt replied that Bill C-9 applied only to the land and that the Inuit still had their native rights to the offshore area. He also explained that extinguishment only applied to certain rights to the land.

On the other hand Quppaq Tayara explained that ITN did not like the agreement. He said that there were three main things they disagreed with in the agreement which are the extinguishment of rights, the receiving of compensation monies for extinguishment, and the selection of different categories of lands. He also stated that if ITN did not get what they were after concerning these three points, they might take the agreement to court in order to get their way. However, he did not explain on what legal grounds that ITN could successfully challenge the James Bay and Northern Québec Agreement in court.

Later in the meeting Charlie Watt pointed out that it would be useless to break the agreement because the Inuit need it right now to build upon. He said this was very important now, especially when the Inuit are trying to give their input into writing a new constitution for Canada. He further explained that many of the things that all Inuit want, including ITN, can only be obtained through changes in the constitution. Charlie Watt finished his argument by saying that if the agreement was broken now, the Inuit would be left with very little because there would still be the constitution that does not recognize the rights of Inuit and there would be no agreement to build upon, or to try to change things with.

Wakeham Bay was the last meeting before Charlie Watt had to leave for his emergency meeting in Montréal. The Makivik officials left at about one o'clock at night and reached Kuujjuaq a couple of hours later.

(Atuaqnik, November 1979, page 12)

"Ai-Yai-Ya!"

Up to 15¢ per square foot Could Lead to Profits for Landholding Corporation
By Willie Adams

Representatives from all the Landholding Corporations met together in Kuujjuaq (Ft. Chimo) from October 1 to 5 to discuss the establishment and operation of these new bodies.

Every community in Northern Québec is supposed to set up it's own Landholding Corporation. All Inuit residents who are beneficiaries of the agreement are members of the Landholding Corporation of his or her community. The members are supposed to elect the board of directors which will make many of the decisions for their Landholding Corporation in their community.

The purpose of these bodies is to do what their names imply. The Landholding Corporations are established to "hold" or "own" the Category I lands in the communities. It is through these bodies that the Inuit of each settlement will jointly own their Category I lands.

The role of each Landholding Corporation is to make decisions on what will happen to the land they own and to ensure that the Inuit will benefit from owning it. Because of this, the Landholding Corporation will be leasing land to many of the organization or companies that may wish to use a block of land within a community. In other words, the Landholding Corporations, especially in the larger settlements will be able to make money from the land leases. At first, the money from this will be used to cover the expenses of operating the corporations, but later when the profits are large enough, the money could be used to start projects or small businesses that will benefit the whole Inuit community.

It was these matters that were discussed at the meeting in Kuujjuaq in October. Since all the communities in Northern Québec (except Ivujivik & Povungnituk) have established their Landholding Corporations, the meeting was well attended by either the president or secretary of the different Landholding Corporations. Generally, the meeting went quite well with everyone becoming more familiar with the responsibilities and operations of these new bodies.

The representatives discussed what kind of leases they could arrange and how much they would charge the different organizations who want to use a block of Category I land. For example, it was suggested that the Landholding Corporations could use the following guidelines when negotiating a lease with an interested person or organization:

Leases for Industrial Operations: 7 ½ to 15 cents per
   square foot per year.
Leases for Commercial Operations: (stores, banks, etc.):
   5 to 12 cents per square foot per year.
Leases for Residential Purposes: 1 to 7 ½ cents per
   square foot per year.

Also discussed was the idea that a lease should only be given for a specific purpose. In other words, if an organization leased land to build residential houses for it's staff, it could not later decide to use the land it leased for an office building.

Generally, all of these questions about how much to lease the land for, and for what purpose the land will be used, will be decided between the board of directors of the Landholding Corporation and the group or person who wants to lease some land in the Category 1 area. In addition it was also recommended that leases lasting more than five years should be decided by the membership in general. Leases for a period of less than five years could be decided by a resolution of the board of directors only.

The Makivik Corporation is also helping out the Landholding Corporations establish their operations. In fact Makivik has set up a six man board called "Kigatuqvik" that will assist the local Landholding Corporation in each of the communities whenever possible. This board will also be involved in matters relating to Category I & II lands under Bill 29 (the provincial law that legally establishes Inuit rights in the different categories of land.)

Furthermore, Makivik's resolution that was passed last June to provide up to a million dollars a year for all of the Landholding Corporations together for five years, means that each corporation should have enough money to get started. The plan is that the million dollars will be divided up among the Landholding Corporations, and that they will be able to use it for such things as hiring an employee or two for their operation. However, a Makivik official stated that money should not only be used for salaries, but also for special projects in communities. Sooner or later, the Landholding Corporations should be able to make enough money to support their own operations and projects from the leases for the land. This will probably be easier for some larger communities because there are usually more organizations that want to establish themselves in these settlements. This means leases and more profits.

Already, Kuujjuaq has started to lease some of its land to organizations that have settled in that community. It won't be long before the other communities are also ready to do the same.

Finally, it was discussed that there should be two people from each Landholding Corporation to have training for three weeks. But there was a slight problem as to how the training would be funded. This was not resolved at this meeting but was going to be researched into by Kigatuqvik.

(Atuaqnik, November 1979, page 17)

$37 Million for Improvements in Northern Québec

By M. McGoldrick

Last May the Québec Government approved an expenditure of $37 million to upgrade sanitary conditions and to provide better municipal (community) services in Northern Québec. This large sum of money will be spent over a period of five years to carry out the necessary improvements in the settlements.

Generally, the $37 million is being made available to cover the usual cost of administration of the community councils and to carry out some recommendation in a special government report about the bad sanitary conditions and the lack of municipal services in the settlements. For example it has been recommended that improved systems of delivering water and collecting sewerage waste be set up in most of the communities. In addition, the money will also be used to help establish needed municipal services such as fire protection, proper access roads, airstrips, community halls, and community council offices.

According to Philippe Nadeau, a Québec Government representative with SAGMAI, the funds mean that the "Québec Government has accepted to spend money on the territory through the public bodies that were negotiated under the agreement," and that they, "are carrying out the philosophy of the agreement."

Philippe said the decision to go ahead and approve the

$37 million budget started last summer when the Québec minister of Social Affairs came up to Fort Chimo for ceremonies at the beginning of the construction of the new Ungava Hospital. At that time the minister saw for himself some of the sanitary conditions in some of the communities and found that they were unacceptable. As a result, he appointed Mr. Jolicoeur to conduct a study to see what could be done to improve things.

Mr. Jolicoeur then went to many of the communities in Northern Québec to see the situation himself. After several months of study, he released his report.

The first part of the report dealt with improving sanitary conditions. The report recommends such things as a clean up campaign for all communities, the continuation of tests in one community of biological toilets to see if it could replace the honey bag system, the closing of existing dumps and the opening of new ones surrounded by fences in better locations, installation of plumbing in all the houses in Northern Québec, additional water and shit trucks or Muskegs for all communities except Great Whale River, Povungnituk, and Kuujjuaq (Chimo), and the construction of public showers and laundries for all communities that do not have them.

The report also stated that water tanks should be installed in the houses in Akulivik, Tasiujak (Leaf Bay), and Aupaluk as soon as possible. It also suggests that some sort of sewage system and water distribution networks consisting of pipes under and over ground be installed in the five larger communities.

The report also makes some obvious recommendations such as the use of stronger honey bags, and that garbage and honey bags should not be left along the streets or around the houses without protection from dogs or accidents.

The second part of the report deals with the question of proper community services (which will soon be known as municipal services) in all the settlements in Northern Québec. It recommends that all communities should have at least one loader, one bulldozer, one snowblower, and a truck or two. The larger communities should have more of these and in addition, a grader or two, and a rock crusher. The larger communities could lend some of their additional equipment to the smaller ones as needed.

The second part of the report indicates that each community should have a properly built road to its local dump, water pump house, gravel pit, and airstrip. Also, the streets within the communities should be improved according to necessary standards and should include ditches for the spring run off.

The report also states that every community should be provided with a proper airstrip that is at least 3,000 feet long, basic fire fighting equipment, a good size community hall, and administrative buildings to provide office space for the councillors, mayor, and the secretary-treasurer of each community.

The total budget for the proposed recommendations is estimated at approximately $37 million. When the Québec Government received the final recommendations it decided to accept them and to approve the necessary funds to carry out many of the proposals. The announcement of this decision by the provincial government reached the Kativik Regional Government offices in mid-May.

Although the report has been accepted and the funds have been approved, it does not mean everything will be acted on in one year. According to the regional government officials, the money will come over a five year period. Furthermore, some of the recommendations may not be carried out completely as indicated because of unforeseen problems. For example, studies show that when plumbing is installed, houses will use about three times more water than before. In other words the communities and the regional government will have to do a fair amount of planning if the $37 million is going to be put to good use.

The Kativik Regional Government says that each community will have to decide on its priorities during each year of the period. With this, the regional government draws up the budgets for all the settlements. It is through these budgets that the communities will receive their share of the $37 million over the next five years.

(Atuaqnik, Summer Issue 1979, page 26)

Imaqpik to Get 147 foot Ship & Halifax Office

By Alec C. Gordon

Imaqpik Fisheries has an agreement to purchase what will be their first fishing vessel and is also going ahead with plans to move its operations office to Halifax, Nova Scotia.

According to Imaqpik Assistant General Manager Tikilie Kleist, they have an agreement to purchase a ship. It is 44.5 meters (147 feet) long, and will accommodate a crew of 19 people and it has the same fishing capacity as the vessel Imaqpik had been leasing. If everything goes as planned, Imaqpik will purchase the ship in Denmark and will take delivery May 31. Mr. Kleist said that they expect that the ship will go into operation between June 1 to 15, and that it will start fishing in the Ungava Bay area. The name they have chosen for their first ship is "Lumaaq."

Mr. Kleist also said that the Imaqpik Board of Directors have decided to move their operations office to Halifax. He explained that the reason for the move to Halifax from Montréal is because, "All the other Canadian fisheries offices are located there." Tikilie also said that it has been costing too much money to travel back and forth between Montréal and Halifax. "It is more economical for Imaqpik to unload in Halifax than it is in Greenland," said Tikilie, adding that shipping is cheaper in Halifax than it is in Greenland.

Although the operations office of Imaqpik will be sta-

tioned in Halifax, its head office will still remain in Kuujjuaq. Tikilie estimated that there would be approximately
5 employees at the operations office including the General
Manager, Neil Greig.

According to Tikilie, Imaqpik's catch of shrimp is doing much better this year than last, and has been averaging
up to 4 tons a day. He said that it is better to catch shrimp
between the months of January and May because of the
better quality when they do not have eggs.

Mr. Kleist also stated that it will probably take up to 5
years until Imaqpik really starts to make profit. He said that
they will be spending to make money, such as their plans to
purchase their ship. Again, Mr. Kleist explained that it will
be less expensive to own a boat rather than chartering it.

So far, the crew from Northern Québec that Imaqpik
has been hiring for the shrimp fisheries have been doing very well. Tikilie said that, "They are some of the best
fishermen in the world," though the Inuit crew have never
been active in deep sea fishing. Tikilie predicted that it
might be a little harder this spring to get a fresh new crew
because many people like to go hunting for themselves
during this time of year. He also stated that the reason why
they change the crews so often is because they eventually want to find out which people are really interested
in becoming full time fishermen. He also said that maybe
these people who enjoy their work in fisheries may one
day want to operate their own fisheries off the Ungava or
Hudson Bay coast.

Tikilie took the opportunity to describe how the employees get paid for working with Imaqpik fisheries, since there has been some confusion over the matter.

The crew is paid after the shrimp catch has been sold to market. Tikilie said that the first crew that was hired for the fisheries have not yet received their final pay. He said, this is because the rest of the catch has not yet been sold. This year Imaqpik guarantees to pay each crew member $6 an hour at 84 hours a week and the employee receives pay every week. The Imaqpik fisheries opens a bank account in Kuujjuaq for their employees that are on the ship and each time it is pay day, the cheques are deposited at the bank in the employees account.

(Atuaqnik, April/May 1980, page 13)

The Co-op Federation Annual Meeting
By Charlie Patsauq

The Federation of Co-ops held its annual meeting from March 17-27, and the usual yearly review of Co-op activities was discussed.

Two delegates from all the communities in Northern Québec except Aupaluk attended the meeting. Most of the delegates found the meeting exhausting with days that often started at 9 o'clock in the morning and ending at 11 o'clock in the evening.

The Federation offices in Montréal are impressive for someone visiting them for the first time. There are many carvings, and still more in the carving bank, which is located in the rear. There is a lot of Inuit art, such as prints, basket weaving, sewing art, and carvings, that are found in abundance in the hallways and rooms. There is also a display room that contains many works, along with another room that is full of thousands of unpacked carvings.

Snowmobile Quality
One of the things that was discussed at the meeting was snowmobile quality. The Federation is no longer selling Ski-doos from Bombardier because it is felt that their new models are not suited for hunting purposes.

Representatives from Bombardier were in attendance at the beginning of the meeting. At that time the Co-op thanked them for giving the Federations credit when it

was just starting and having a difficult time. However, the President of the Federation, Pauloosie Kadsudluak, informed the Bomdardier people that their 1980 models are inferior for the Inuit. But he assured them that when Bombardier starts to make better Ski-doos, there will be a standing market in Northern Québec.

David Naalatik said that "what Bombardier makes now is useless for hunting." The Federation will not buy Bombardier products until they come up with something better for the Inuit. Because of this, the Federation switched from Bomdardier to John Deere.

Representatives from John Deere were also attending the meeting. They received a number of suggestions from the delegates about modifying their machines for Northern conditions. As a result, John Deere will be making some modifications according to Inuit suggestions.

Already one such machine is being tested in Inukjuak. That snowmobile is a new model called "WorkFire," and has been designed with many Inuit suggestions. In addition, John Deere will continue to make modifications according to Inuit suggestions.

Sealift & Facilities

The sealift problems were discussed at this meeting. Apparently there are problems with the sealifts every year and the delegates at the meeting outlined many of them. The Federation said that it would try to solve these problems in the future.

In addition, there was the Co-op review settlement by

settlement for the year 1979. Some of the individual Co-ops made a profit, and some didn't.

At this meeting, the community Co-ops presented their need for facilities one by one. The meeting focused on the ones that needed them the most, and thus set their priorities. They also had to consider the requests from the year before that could not be met at that time. When the people decided who was to get what, everyone seems satisfied with the priorities and supported them.

Generally, the Co-ops asked for renovations, warehouses, and transportation facilities. The Co-ops receiving such facilities will try to come up with a way to help pay for some of the cost.

Carvings
One of the more interesting parts of the meeting was the discussion on carvings.

Generally, sales were up with the carvings of the Inuit of Northern Québec. And Inukjuak was responsible for the largest share of the carvings sold—42% was the figure given at the meeting for Inukjuak's share.

The delegates were told that Inuit will have to be very careful about bad carvings because these could ruin the market. It was said that there has to be quality control.

Low quality carvings was not the only problem. The overpricing of carvings was also part of it.

In order to overcome these problems, the delegates passed a motion to send back carvings so that the purchasing managers will learn how to avoid over pricing carvings

or buying bad ones.

Another factor that affected carvings was that bone carvings are difficult, if not impossible, to sell in the United States. This is because that country is boycotting bone carvings because they feel this can help save certain animals.

The selling of soapstone was also one of the topics covered at the meeting. The delegates made it clear that if any soapstone is to be sold to another community, the soapstone will have to be of good quality, otherwise, the purpose of the whole project is defeated. They agreed that good stone will have to be sold if it is going to be meaningful.

There was also a suggestion that the Federation consider buying a Peterhead boat so that it could transport soapstone to the communities for sale. At the moment it is not known what is being done about this.

It was reported that 300 stores in Canada, 104 stores in the US and 13 stores in Europe bought carvings from the Federation in 1979.

Another idea that is only a suggestion at the moment is that the Federation open another outlet in addition to the one they have in Montréal. However, more studies will be needed on this matter and consideration will have to be given on the best location for such an outlet. For example, it could be located in the United States, in Europe, or again in southern Canada.

Other Projects

The Co-ops also talked about a number of other projects. One of these is the renting out of canoes.

They thought that the Co-op should rent out canoes, but that they will have to be careful with the canoes they rent out. The individual Co-ops will decide on the matter themselves, but the canoes will have to last longer than a year to ensure good business. It was also pointed out that thought will have to be given to potential problems such as what will happen if a canoe was broken.

In addition, they considered renting radios, and again, the Co-ops in the communities must decide for themselves.

Another interesting project was a mussel cannery. Wakeham Bay is thinking of this. Mussels are in demand in the other communities, but as they spoil easily, a canning operation is being thought of. However, more research and discussion will be needed.

Still another project that was talked about was Puktuugs (seal meat & fat inside a seal skin). Many people like puktuugs and some people are thinking about selling this locally. It was said that it should first be experimental for a year, and if successful, it should be considered a business.

It was mentioned that it is stated in the Federation Charter that the Co-ops could operate the community or municipal services. At the moment, these services are handled by the local corporations or the new municipal governments. If the Co-ops want to provide some of these services, they will have to deal with these bodies.

At the federation meeting, Thomassie Qumak from Povungnituk informed the meeting that the Povungnituk Co-op would be taking back their profits. They plan to use these profits to help Inuit Tungavingat Nunaminni (ITN) take the Makivik Corporation to court over the agreement. They plan to take their profits back in installments because they realize that the money is used to help out other Co-ops who may not be doing so well.

Elections

Elections were held towards the end of the meeting. These are the present executives: Pauloosie Kadsudluak, Annie Tulugak, Bobby Snowball, Davidee Naalatik, Joanasie Ningiuk. At the meeting they elected more directors for the federation. These people were elected: Matusie Amagoalik from Povungnituk, Pauloosie Napartuk from Kuujuarapik, Steven Shem from Kuujuarpik (Crée), Charlie Mark from Ivujivik, Ohituk Amamatuak from Salluit, Eli Elijasiapik from Inukjuak, Tommy Johannes from Kuujjuaq, Willie Etok from Kangirsualukjuak, Thomisa Thomassie from Kangirsuk, Naala Napaluk from Kangirsujuak, Markusiapik Anautak from Akulivik and Wemindji only has visitor status.

(Atuaqnik, April/May 1980, page 15)

Inuit Leasing Flying into Profits
By William Tagoona

Inuit Leasing, a subsidiary company of Makivik, says for the last quarter of their year they've turned a profit of $30,000 and have set a goal to make a net profit of $500,000 in their coming year.

Inuit Leasing is a company which buys and sells aircrafts. They also operate 2 King Air aircrafts for chartered or contract work.

The company was originally formed to operate Makivik's King Air and to generate a little income to offset the cost of using the aircraft. Then a little over a year ago the Makivik board decided to try and develop it into a profit making company.

George Simon, Vice President, said the company has sold three aircrafts this year. One to Labrador Airways, one to an American company, and a Twin Otter to Air Inuit (on the sale to Air Inuit they did not make any profit, in fact, they took a loss). He said to benefit an affiliate company, they did not take any profit.

"In the past year we've had 2 very big contracts, one out of Newfoundland and one out of Calgary," said Mr. Simon. There are other possible contracts which are still in the negotiation stage. He said, "We're working on a couple of contracts, one out of Mexico and another somewhere else."

Last September Inuit Leasing made a successful Medivac from Igloolik to Montréal. The Frobisher hospital was impressed with the aircraft used and later requested a meeting with the company.

"We're still negotiating with the hospital in Frobisher to base a King Air, specially equipped for Medivacs, out of Frobisher. There has been nothing definite decided yet," said Simon. Inuit Leasing would like to see letters of support from the NWT communities sent to the hospital in Frobisher. If the hospital signs a contract with Inuit Leasing then the King Air would become easily accessible to the Ungava Hospital in an emergency.

Over the period of next year Inuit Leasing will be obtaining their own license to run an air service on a chartered basis. Presently Inuit Leasing is operated by another company's license. Therefore, it is putting in a certain amount of money to that company. Mr. Simon feels Inuit Leasing has been very lucky this year. "Usually a company such as this doesn't make profit for about two years, but in our last quarter we've been pretty lucky," said Simon.

The company is also looking at selling one of it's aircrafts which would put the company into a profitable position. "It's not that the company is physically losing money," said Simon, "it's just that when you purchase aircrafts, or any large assets, you have what you call depreciation, which is just a paper figure. It appears though the company is losing money until it liquidates one of those assets. As soon as you liquidate one of those assets it turns a loss into profit."

(Atuaqnik, February 1980, page 5)

Kigiak—On the Move

Kigiak is now in its second year of operations. It has constantly tried to expand its operations and to increase its sources to different agencies and to the local population in Fort Chimo.

The name Kigiak is well known, but not everyone realizes that it is divided into three subsidiaries: Kigiak Builders, Kigiak Maintenance, and Kigiak Fuel Distributors.

Kigiak Builders is the busiest of the three divisions, it has more than twenty employees. So far it has completed construction on two bungalows, one fourplex, one sixplex, the Cape Breton bunk house and the Service Center, all located in Kuujjuaq. These projects have a value of approximately two million dollars.

Presently Kigiak is building a motel (twenty rooms with a bar and restaurant), and a staff house for Air Inuit. Kigiak Builders are also converting the present Air Inuit staff house into a warehouse. Kigiak also has been doing some salvage operations on Pio Lake for an Ontario based company.

Kigiak is already working on proposals for projects for next year. Possible projects could be located in Inukjuak, Kangiasuk, Aupaluk and Kuujjuaaq.

Kigiak Maintenance is involved in repairs and maintenance of buildings and facilities in Kuujjuaq. Plumbing, electrical maintenance and metal work are all part of Kigiak Maintenance. It was originally located in the Arenco

Station but now is in the process of moving into its new building, the Service Center in Kuujjuaq. Kigiak does work for all the different organizations on a fee per call basis.

The new service center offers many new possibilities. It will have individual workshops for plumbing, electrical work, carpentry and metal work. Also in the new building are four service bays for all Kigiak construction and service vehicles.

This center is the only one of its kind in operation in Northern Québec.

The third subsidiary is Kigiak Fuel Distributors, this subsidiary is just starting its second year. It also will be located in the Service Center. Kigiak Fuel Distributors is responsible for the distribution of all petroleum products in Fort Chimo. As it is the newest subsidiary, it is still planning its growth and development.

(Makivik News, November 1980, page 4)

New Five-Year Plan:
Where Your Money Goes
By François Girard

Community representatives made a number of very significant decisions in September, at the Tasiujaq Board meeting of Makivik. Important to many employees of both Makivik and its subsidiaries—whose life will be changed following the most recent budget cuts, but also to all the Inuit, as new financial guidelines have been adopted.

There is now a clear message: the Inuit members, at the community level, need more funds for venture capital and for community development projects.

There has been an overall success in reaching the objectives of the first five year plan established in 1982-83. Sound administrative practices have been reestablished and the net worth of the Corporation (not including compensation money) has dramatically increased.

Measures are being taken to channel a much larger proportion of the net income into tangible benefits, as many were viewing Makivik's bureaucracy as an insatiable beast thriving on any cash surplus available.

As a first approach to these complex matters, I will review the meaning of the newly adopted five year plan under four headings, listing four general concerns for who would end up with $90 million to invest for the present and future generations.

1. Protect the Capital

In 1986–87, almost as much money ($579,000) will go to reinstate the capital of Makivik as during the three first years of the original 5 year plan. The financial mistakes of the first few years are a heavy burden and the faster this money will be back into the Corporation's total worth, the better.

According to the available figures concerning the fore-seen revenues and projected expenses, over $5 million will have been allocated for that purpose at the end of 1991. The Board of Directors has decided to go on with its past decision to "freeze" 20% of the net income of each year for reinstatement of capital.

We must point out that the revenues of Air Inuit are not part of such calculations: A fixed amount has been used in the five year plan in the revenue column (namely $100,000 yearly as management fees).

2. Meet the Inflation Rate

Money sitting idle would quickly loose its purchasing power and must be re-invested. There is a clause in the James Bay Agreement and the laws that followed it, restricting the use of 75% of the compensation monies received to safe, short-term—but less productive—investments. Next November, this restriction will decrease to 50% and therefore more of the compensation monies will be really available for more money-making ventures. All such restrictions cease only in 1997.

Therefore, there are now new means of investing into middle sized and established businesses to obtain significant annual incomes to cope with the inflation rate. For instance, the yearly amount unrestricted by law will increase from the level of $9.9 million to $23.8 million in 1991.

3. Revenues for the Present

There are a number of choices you can make when running a business. For instance, you can use the revenues to finance your cash shortages in the next year. On the other hand, you can let the cash shortages reduce your total possible expenses in the next year and keep your revenues to improve your assets. That is what the five year plan will do.

All the net income (after deduction of the reinstatement of capital) will go into community development projects and new business ventures.

At present the total amount going to such purposes is less than one half of the operating costs of Makivik. In 1991, both amounts would be almost equal. Money for communities or small businesses would reach almost double the level foreseen for the 1986-87 fiscal year in 1991 ($4.4 million as compared to $2.3).

4. Keep Growing

Growth will be found in the total available capital and community projects instead of in the operations and services of Makivik. Beginning this year, the operations will have to remain at the same level unless alternate sources of funding are found, on a project-by-project basis.

Changes in the level of core funding (presently $300,000 a year), and outside funding for research, economic development and communications are the only means of developing the present activities of Makivik in the political, economical and cultural fields.

The total amount of venture capital would reach, in 1991, a level of five times the amount budgeted in 1985-86. Obviously, the Corporation is rapidly changing from the inside, to cope with such challenges.

(Makivik News, December 1986–January 1987, page 19)

Seaku's Commercial and Development Programs Well Underway
By Dave Gillis

Seaku Fisheries commercial fishing operations and development program for the 1987–1988 season are well underway.

The regional fishery received a boost this spring when the Minister of Fisheries and Oceans granted a joint license for northern shrimp to Seaku and Qiqiqtaaluk Corporation of Baffin Island. This should bring the number of vessels fishing for Seaku Fisheries in northern Canadian waters to three; one for each of the two shrimp licenses and a third vessel to harvest Greenland halibut on behalf of Killiniq Fisheries Inc. Approval for this last operation is pending.

Inuit Fishermen Wanted
This situation creates the need for as many as 25 Northern Québec fishermen to fill positions on these vessels, between now and next winter. Seaku, and it's operation partner, Farocan, are currently recruiting interested applicants for these positions. Each trip would last for between two and three months at sea. A "Regional Fishermen's Application Kit" may be obtained from the community council office in any Northern Québec community except Kuujjuaq, where these kits are available at Makivik's Head Office.

Each kit contains a full explanation (English/Inuktitut) of the job and conditions at sea, the terms of employment, a job application form and a passport application form. Interested fishermen should return the completed forms to Seaku Fisheries.

Profits Redirected into Fisheries Development
Profits from 1986-87 regional commercial fisheries are now being redirected back into fishery development projects in Northern Québec. The 1987-88 development program recently approved identified the following projects to be undertaken or continued in the coming year:

- The formulation of a detailed development plan for Seaku which will identify those resources to be given priority in order to 1) expand and stabilize Seaku's regional commercial operations and 2) guide Seaku in its efforts to assist proponents in the domestic sector.
- An exploratory and test-commercial fishing survey for Iceland scallops in the offshore waters of Ungava Bay and Hudson Strait; to be undertaken as a joint project with Qiqiqtaaluq Corporation of Baffin Island.
- The completion of the Arctic Char Migratory Enhancement Test Project at Tasiujaq. Seaku will contribute about 50% of the funding.
- Participation in the Department of Fisheries and Oceans' upcoming (August–September, 1987)

fisheries research cruise; Seaku will send one
biologist/observer.
-Re-activation of the inshore Iceland scallop fishery
development program, to identify and make
arrangements to undertake the next step in this
process, in the 1988 season.
-A pre-feasibility study of the potential for and effects
of fish culture in Northern Québec. This study will
only commence later in the year depending on the
funds available.

Some of this project work will be commissioned to the
Research Department of Makivik and the balance will be
completed by personnel attached directly to Seaku Fisheries. Updates on the progress and results of these development projects and Seaku's regional fishery operations will
appear in future issues of *Makivik News*.

(Makivik News, Spring 1987, page 25)

Action Plan Towards Self-Reliance: Makivik's Project Accepted

As an update of last month's report in Makivik News, we are proud to announce that the proposal to the Native Economic Development Program has been accepted. At this step, let us clarify certain aspects of this project.

by Bruno Pilozzi

At long last, our proposal to establish an Inuit Development Corporation has been approved by the Board of Directors of this federal program.

As mentioned in our previous article, Makivik has accepted the NEDP requirement that Inuit agencies involved in economic development in Northern Québec agree on a single corporate vehicle to administer all loan funds for the development of small businesses. This would include the Inuit Loan Fund and the LEAD Corporation presently under development.

The project consists of a 7 to 9 month development phase to create an Economic Development Corporation for the Inuit of Northern Québec. The envisaged Economic Development Corporation will include the following components:

-development and advisory services;
-small business loan fund (offering loans, loan
   guarantees and financial contributions);
-institutional loans;

-strategic investments: commercialization of
caribou meat; sea transportation; air transportation.

We see a full team of support and advisory staff located
in the communities (6 development officers and 2 senior
analysts); it is felt that lack of information on available help
and incapacity of government agencies to actively assist in
the development of proposals on site are responsible for the
slow growth of business opportunities. These development
officers would be responsible for community animation,
management training and project development.

Proposed Structure of the Development Corporation

While details need to be confirmed following community consultation, the Development Corporation proposed
would not be a subsidiary of the applicant (Makivik) but
a new corporation, independent of any existing organization. It is understood that this structure would be designed
to avoid political influence and stress technical and financial expertise at the operational and decision making levels.

It is contemplated that major northern organizations
with an impact on development of small businesses may be
invited to be present at the Board of Directors: this would
include Makivik, Kativik Regional Development Council
and the Federation of Co-operatives of Northern Québec.

A clearer definition of the roles and responsibilities
of the development and advisory services would need to
be produced during the development phase. Makivik has
been advised by NEDP that the projected advisory service

would need to be scaled down and, should management services be required, a strategy for long-term funding of these activities would need to be developed.

Small Business Loan Fund

Estimates of the need for a small business loan fund of $3.2 million are based on DIAND's evaluation of the total value of unprocessed requests for funding for commercial projects. Available sources of funding presently include the Inuit Loan Fund due to be transferred to the Inuit and a LEAD Corporation presently under development. The need for a loan fund for small business development would need to be established in a more rigorous manner during the initial phase.

Institutional Loans

The institutional loan component and strategic investments play a critical role in the context of an Inuit development corporation: The creation of small businesses in Northern Québec faces major risk factors due to limited management and business expertise, high transportation costs, limited communication networks and absence of banking services. The business potential is not at present sufficiently varied across communities or industrial sectors to permit a reasonable investment mix. To offset the higher risks inherent to a northern loan fund and produce interest revenues sufficient to cover the high cost of the advisory services needed to stimulate the development of small businesses, a measure of stabilization factor had to be

built into the project. The relatively safe operation of institutional loans (school board, health board and hospitals, re
gional government) has been included to provide for this.

This institutional loan fund is evaluated at $2.5 million
and will only provide guaranteed short-term loans. It is
planned that, as needs for a small business development
fund increase in the future and that better diversification
of loan risks become possible, this fund will be transferred
to the small business development fund.

Strategic Investments

The strategic investments have been selected to reflect
the need for tighter Inuit control on the transportation
costs that are vital to the development of businesses in the
North while providing guaranteed annual revenues. The
commercialization of caribou meat, made possible by recent provincial legislation changes, deals with a new industry using a community resource.

The scope of the currently contemplated strategic investments are as follows:

Sea transportation (sea-lift): $2.1 million
Commercialization of caribou meat: $1.2 million
Air transportation expansion: $1.0 million

The acquisition of Shell Canada tank farms was included by Makivik as a possible strategic investment; since an
independent proposal presented to NEDP by the Federation of Co-ops concerns the same activity, this has been left
out in the present recommendation. However, an agree-

ment has been reached: If NEDP finances the FCNQ's bid to purchase the Shell tank farms, then such a loan to them would become repayable to the proposed Inuit Development Corporation as one of its strategic investments.

It must be noted that DIAND is exploring the possibility of a transfer to a northern institution of the Inuit Loan Fund (technical problems concerning the loan guarantee section and the transferability of repayment of outstanding accounts of this fund need to be solved before this can be done). Consultations with DIAND indicate that the Inuit Loan Fund may not be viable as a stand alone fund; it is expected that the Development Corporation would be the beneficiary of such a transfer, and project activities include negotiations to this effect.

A CEIC funded feasibility phase for a LEAD Corporation is presently under way with closely related objectives; it is a requirement of the present recommendation that Makivik explore the possibilities for a merger of these two closely related activities in order to avoid duplication and optimize the use of government funds in the support of small business development.

CEIC has approached NEDP with regard to possible joint-funding of the LEAD Corporation and has indicated that LEAD would consider funding operational costs of the institution, but would require their LEAD project to explore the possibility of a merger with the projected Makivik sponsored institution.

(Makivik News, February 1987, page 9)

Transfer for Pitaqvik

Aupaluk's Pitaqvik General Store has been trying to join the FCNQ network for more than a year. The store, established several years ago by Aupaluk's Landholding Corporation, experienced early financial difficulties but now generates a healthy annual profit.

Agreement has finally been reached between the Landholding Corporation, the community of Aupaluk, Makivik, and FCNQ, whereby the Federation will now take over Pitaqvik and run it as a new Co-Op. This agreement follows intensive discussions at Makivik's Tasiujaq AGM in March, and formal acceptance of the plan at the FCNQ's AGM in Kangiqsujuaq.

FCNQ sent Peter Murdoch to Aupaluk in late May to assess the store's inventory, and to negotiate the takeover. The FCNQ preferred not to purchase the current store building. Through negotiation, they agreed to rent the old store building for one year while the Aupaluk Co-Op constructs a new building. Aupaluk's Landholding Corporation plans to use the old building for some other purpose.

Everyone supports Aupaluk's desire to become a member of the FCNQ network. Makivik recognizes that operating a community general store is not part of its mandate. Makivik originally got involved in financial and technical support of Pitaqvik's operations. However, some people have been concerned that Makivik is now giving up a growing business.

Makivik director Johnny Appaahattak said, "The main reason why we want the FCNQ to take over our store is because the store charges such high prices. The FCNQ can take over the store and lower the profit margin. Aupaluk people are not able to continue paying the high prices."

President Charlie Watt feels that, when Pitaqvik is transferred to the FCNQ, Makivik should recover the outstanding loans it made to the store.

Peter Murdoch told *Makivik News* that the new Co-Op will have the same advantages and responsibilities as all the other members of the FCNQ network. He says that better service and lower prices will result.

"If they would like to plan for other economic development," said Murdoch, "Aupaluk will have the same opportunities as all the other Co-ops in Northern Québec." This could include the purchasing and marketing of Inuit art, sewing programs, and tourism development.

Makivik, Aupaluk's Landholding Corporation, and the Federation hope for a smooth transfer of administrations. Understanding between all parties will help to implement this long awaited agreement.

(Makivik News, June 1988, page 21)

Minnie Grey Talks About Nunavik's Economy

Makivik News: In your opinion, what part should Makivik play in the economic development of Nunavik?

Minnie Grey: Makivik is supposed to be promoting economic development and creating subsidiaries, such as Air Inuit. But I also think that Makivik should be trying to be directly involved with the communities efforts, as far as investing directly into community benefits. I think money should be invested into the communities whenever possible, through the Landholding Corporations, as has been happening lately.

Makivik News: What efforts can be made by Inuit at the community level?

Minnie Grey: Makivik's purpose is to make sure that everybody, collectively, benefits. It's in the Charter. Where the Landholding Corporations and the Municipal Corporations, the Co-op, or anybody else in the community knows the community's needs, it's up to them to think of a way to benefit their community as far as projects or any kind of economic development is concerned.

Makivik News: Have the communities been taking full advantage of Makivik's Community Development Fund (CDF)?

Minnie Grey: They're starting to see it as something that they can take advantage of. It's been going on for the past three years, this fund, but it's only recently that certain

Landholding Corporations are starting to use the money to develop themselves.

Makivik News: What would you like to see the CDF used for by communities? What kinds of projects or opportunities?

Minnie Grey: Take Quaqtaq, for example. The Landholding Corporation of Quaqtaq wants to start a garment (clothing) industry—down parkas, etc.—which will create jobs locally, and they need buildings to set up the company. They've come to Makivik and asked for money, which has been granted, to buy trailers. Things like that, where the Landholding Corporation gains some assets so that they can start a business that is known by the people, such as the garment industry, which will be creating jobs for women.

Ski-doos are always needed. Instead of the Co-op or the Bay doing it, the Landholding Corporations started snowmobile dealerships. One particular community was granted some money from Makivik to buy the machines. I really feel that there's a lot of opportunity, if you just take things that people need in the community, and try to promote it.

In the past there was a lot of skepticism about granting money to the communities, but after a few years of nothing happening, Makivik has turned around and said, "Look, if it's going to benefit the community as a whole, if the Landholding Corporation has a good idea, we have no problem in granting money or even a loan." That's what the money is for.

Makivik News: Inukjuak's arena was supposed to be a

model for future arenas in Nunavik. Will we soon see more arenas, or other facilities?

Minnie Grey: I am in the process of making a proposal to the Board of Directors as to what steps should be taken to continue this program. I feel very strongly that the communities are right in saying that they need recreational facilities, whether an arena or a proper building. I'm getting very concerned about it.

Makivik has the money, as least as a contribution. We've asked KRG, as the body responsible for recreation, to come up with a list where they show which communities should have recreational facilities first. They've recently done a study and we're supposed to go to the government and convince them to start a five year program.

Makivik News: You are now working on projects towards bringing banking services to the North, and promoting tourism in Nunavik. How close to success are these projects, and when can Inuit expect to see some results?

Minnie Grey: Makivik's new approach to tourism is to find partners for joint ventures to take over outfitting and promote tourism. We'll be hiring somebody specifically to be looking after that.

Banking is a totally different thing. We had a study done, but we just haven't had the time to look at it. There have been a few approaches to different banks.

Makivik News: Finally, what is it like being the only female Makivik executive? What would you say to other Inuit women who may be thinking about participating in Nunavik politics?

Minnie Grey: They have to have a lot of patience! Especially if they have children. But I think that women are much more sensitive to needs and realities.

Makivik News: Thank you for this interview, Minnie.

(Makivik News, December 1988, page 13)

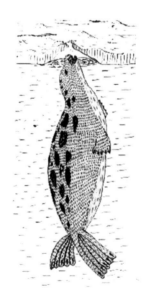

Quaqtaq Parka Industry Takes Shape

Quaqtaq's Tuvaaluk Landholding Corporation is working to start a down parka manufacturing industry. Quaqtaq is already well known for the high quality goose down parkas made privately by local seamstresses.

The industry is expected to boost the local economy significantly. Tuvaaluk's plan provides for a program to train six women in the first year. Four more trainees will be added in the following two years. They will be taught the basics of the industry, using domestic sewing machines. They will also be taught how to run and manage such an industry. Industrial equipment will be brought in for the final training in a factory-type atmosphere.

Makivik has helped Tuvaaluk buy three trailers left by an airstrip construction company, to house the proposed parka industry. Funding for the purchase and renovation of these trailers was provided by Makivik's Community Development Fund (CDF). There are plans to secure further funding from Canadian government agencies to develop the training program.

Truly Inuit Parkas

Inuit-style parkas are becoming more popular down south, but are usually designed and made there. A truly Inuit parka from the North should have great appeal to southern buyers.

The parkas will be manufactured from fabric pre-cut to

southern specifications by southern cutters. The pieces will be sent to Quaqtaq for sewing, and goose or duck down will be used as insulation. Artistic designs will also be sewn on the outer shell.

Local Industry has Reputation

Tuvaaluk president Bob Deere told *Makivik News* that, "These women have managed to establish an excellent reputation for making fine parkas. Our efforts now are for the support and development of an already reputable local industry."

The parkas will be sold in Nunavik during the first year. Air Inuit and Hydro-Québec are interested in buying made to order parkas. Tuvaaluk hopes to sell parkas to major southern stores in the second year of operation.

If the industry grows successfully, and depending on demand for the parkas, Quaqtaq may turn to other communities for supplies of down and fox furs. Meanwhile, Tuvaaluk is confident that their Inuit parkas will sell well. They plan to appeal to southern buyers as their major market.

(Makivik News, October 1988, page 21)

New Directions for Economic Development

Among the many issues discussed at the Inukjuak Annual General Meeting (AGM), the need for growth in Nunavik's economy was one of the most important. The meeting agreed that a wide range of commercial activities are needed to provide jobs for the largely unemployed Inuit population.

Each community has unique qualities particular to that part of Nunavik. A complete study of each community may be needed to choose commercial activities that are viable. When the particular strengths and weaknesses of each community are identified, proper economic policies can be planned where there have been none until now.

Potential areas of employment development for all sectors of the population were discussed at the AGM. Hunters and fishermen, graduates, and school dropouts were all considered in the workshop discussions about possible new fields for jobs creation.

Landholding Services to KRDC

Minnie Grey, then Makivik's Vice-President for Community and Economic Development, led the workshop on economic development. She announced that Makivik is transferring to the Kativik Regional Development Council (KRDC) the services Makivik has provided to Landholding Corporations. Makivik will give $137,000 to KRDC to help the early stages of the transfer. KRDC will

now provide the consulting and accounting services which Landholding Corporations and other organizations need.

Previously, KRDC had concentrated on providing assistance to individual entrepreneurs, while Makivik's Community and Economic Development Department (CEDD) served the Landholding Corporations. However, because KRDC and Makivik's responsibilities tended to overlap, it was agreed that Makivik would transfer its services to KRDC. Makivik continues to oversee legal services to Landholding Corporations, a responsibility identified in the James Bay and Northern Québec Agreement (JBNQA).

KRDC has also received $3.59 million from the Native Economic Development Program (NEDP). These funds are to provide project development and assistance to group and individual entrepreneurs. The money will be administered by the Kativik Investment Fund, which provides business loans.

KRDC was established in 1980 as the preferential consulting body of the Economic Planning and Development Office of Québec (OPDQ). It is presently funded by OPDQ, the federal government, and Makivik.

Development by Joint Ventures

With the arrival of Mark T. Gordon as Third Vice-President of Makivik, the Community and Economic Development Department (CEDD) has assumed a new mandate.

The CEDD will now study ways to stimulate the Nunavik economy and will identify areas where Makivik may establish infrastructures needed for businesses. The emphasis will be on manufacturing and service industry development at the community level, using funds generated by Makivik's earnings. These moves will aim to reduce the massive flow of money to the south, a reality which affects the health of Nunavik's economy.

Makivik's CEDD will lobby the federal and provincial governments to lift restrictions on the development of Nunavik's renewable resources. The CEDD will also look at ways for Nunavik businesses to reach Canadian and international markets for joint ventures in tourism, marketing, purchasing, construction, and transportation.

(Makivik News, June 1989, page 17)

New Markets for Furs?

In response to drastic drops in fur prices during the past ten years, Makivik is studying ways of developing commercial markets for Nunavik hunters and trappers.

Fur and skin prices are depressed worldwide. Projects designed for Inuit hunters and trappers will have to provide reliable long-term markets for furs and skins.

Fur "farming" or ranching schemes are foreign to Inuit, so these possibilities have yet to be explored in Nunavik. A Makivik sponsored study judged that full-scale fox farming is not economically feasible now, although limited opportunities exist for ranching high priced furs such as marten and sable.

The FCNQ Fur Department sells skins received from Nunavik Co-ops at the annual Hudson Bay Company fur auction. The only furs selling well are marten from the Kuujjuaq area, red fox, bear, and wolf skins. White fox and sealskins are not selling well right now.

Because the FCNQ sells only a small quantity of furs, the Federation is not actively looking for new markets. However, if a new skin or fur product were created by Inuit (like the popular ookpik doll created by Jeannie Snowball of Kuujjuaq in the early 1970s) then there may be opportunities for processed skin items.

A professional tanner has been contracted by the FCNQ and KSB to teach southern tanning methods in Nunavik. Inuit can use these new methods to produce better skins for clothing or handicrafts, and should try to learn more about designing and preparing skin goods for southern markets. There has been limited success in selling sealskin garments and leather goods made from dyed or de-haired skins from other parts of Canada.

Southern tanners and fashion designers have said that sealskin is one of the finest leathers in the world. However, demand for sealskin is very low, so the key to successful marketing is producing exciting products.

NWT government programs have been set up to buy sealskins, but the prices paid do not reflect true world value. This solution cannot provide long-term security for hunters and trappers.

Amiq Fine Leathers, a company owned by the Inuit of NWT, produces and sells sealskin and fish skin wallets, purses, and bags to southern stores. They have also recently started making sealskin jackets.

Amiq was set up by Nunasi Corporation when the price of sealskins dropped drastically and NWT hunters could no longer earn a living. The primary reason for establishing Amiq Fine Leathers was to provide a market for NWT hunters' sealskins. However, it is not clear yet whether Amiq is a profitable enterprise.

While their market is now limited to Canada, Amiq has plans to expand internationally and is looking for buyers in the Orient.

(Makivik News, September 1989, page 25)

Competition for Banking Services

A study is being conducted into the possibility of bringing more banking services to Nunavik's communities with the help of Kativik Regional Development Council (KRDC) and Makivik Corporation.

Since the 1970s, Kuujjuaq has been the only Nunavik community able to sustain a bank, a branch of the Canadian Imperial Bank of Commerce (CIBC).

CIBC says it serves customers throughout Nunavik long distance, including for loans. To get a loan a person must be a bank client for six months and be employed at a full-time job for at least nine months. Any CIBC customer in Nunavik can do their banking by telephone or fax. The bank also serves many of Nunavik's municipal corporations.

However, according to Makivik 3rd Vice-President Mark T. Gordon, Kuujjuaq's population isn't satisfied with the local CIBC services. Gordon says that Kuujjuaq, Salluit, and Inukjuak or Povungnituk are being considered by the Caisse Populaire, a Québec based Co-operative bank, for future northern branches.

"They don't want to set up an office in any Nunavik communities if they (the bank) aren't going to gain from it," he says. The Caisse Populaire wants to set up first in Kuujjuaq because it feels that is the ideal location.

Who Needs Another Bank?

Monique Brunei, Kuujjuaq's CIBC manager, agrees Nunavik needs more banks, especially on the Hudson Bay coast and in one of the upper Ungava communities. But Brunei doesn't think having two banks in Kuujjuaq is a good idea because, "it will create unnecessary competition for such a small place." During a recent meeting of Makivik's Board of Directors it was agreed that the Caisse Populaire shouldn't try to get established in Kuujjuaq.

Caisse Populaire claims their bank would be controlled by the community, while all decisions concerning CIBC banking operations are resolved in the south.

"Money would stay in the community," says Jocelyn Geoffroi, vice-president of the Caisse Populaire for the Abitibi region. "Members would also have the opportunity to vote for their own board of directors."

Geoffroi says any member would automatically become a shareholder, and that Kuujjuaq is indeed the best choice for a new branch: "But it will be up to the people where we will establish."

Kuujjuaq and Kuujjuaraapik Take Action

KRDC informed the Nunavik communities that they should produce surveys of their residents' financial status and sign petitions if they want local banks established.

"The people of Kuujjuaq have done just that and have clearly shown they want Caisse Populaire in their community," says KRDC's Jean-Guy Bousquet. KRDC is hoping to have a final proposal on banks ready for Makivik's Annual General Meeting this spring.

It is believed that the Crée community at Great Whale River is also considering a Caisse Populaire operation to satisfy their banking needs. Kuujjuaraapik's Makivik representative Charlie Kowcharlie says if the Crée plan doesn't go through, the Inuit will be asking Makivik to help establish a local branch.

"We have been wanting a bank in our community for quite some time," Kowcharlie says.

(Makivik News, January 1991, page 27)

Inuksiutiit: A Private Business
By Johnny Peters, as presented at the AGM

Inuksiutiit Country Food Store

Over the years that I have worked in the enhancement of wildlife and its commercial utilization, I have found that I have not lost my traditional ways of hunting and fishing in my Inuk land. I have been operating a commercial country food store in Kuujjuaq for the past two years, and the food I serve at my store is treated with the same care as the food I eat at my home, the same way my ancestors and yours used to eat.

Business in a country food store is mainly for Inuit. I am concerned about the legislation governing us and this is why I am here today.

I seek support for the regional use of country food stores as a means of ensuring fresh stocks of food to the communities and to generate employment.

As the caribou herd displaces itself to other communities, Kuujjuaq will one day become a consumer of caribou, when its capacity to harvest the herd ceases to exist. Other communities must then take over to ensure our supply.

Other than that, I personally feel strongly that hunting and fishing must be carried on in order to ensure our traditions and culture. If we change our food and eating habits, we change our culture.

Maintaining hunting and fishing is a must. But their survival as economic activities must be supported on a regional basis. This is not to make the Hunter Support Program redundant. On the contrary, I am promoting a complementary activity rooted in our traditions.

Many people my age have jobs; jobs that they would gladly give up if they could earn a living with their traditional skills. I therefore feel that we should encourage the employment of our seniors that can still practice the traditional skills of hunting and fishing. I ask for support for this. We need financial assistance to support a program aimed at employment in the utilization of our renewable resources. Due to the complexity of setting up of such an industry such as transportation logistics, standards and inspections, we have to foresee a duration of five years for this program. I would go further as to suggest that we encourage an income security program to launch this industry. I am prepared to assume that other costs be covered by the commercial aspect of the program.

I have proven to myself that a country food store can operate profitably throughout the region. Therefore, I think that we should promote the utilization of country food as an industry. We are still far behind our relatives in other arctic countries.

I therefore suggest resolutions today to: 1) Support the commercialization of our renewable resources. 2) Mandate our regional organizations to secure the financial resources to support the employment costs of a regional country food development program.

Makivik's Investments

Some of Makivik's investments are fairly obvious: the subsidiaries. In fact, 20% of the Investment fund has been used to purchase, or develop subsidiaries like the airlines, fisheries, and travel agent. The bulk of the investment fund—over $81 million (71.2% of the Initial and JBNQA Implementation Fund) is invested in stocks, bonds, and the money markets.

Willie Watt—Makivik's Treasurer—presides over a considerable investment portfolio. *Makivik News* spoke to Willie Watt and members of his staff about the fund. We wondered, for example, how Makivik picks its stocks to invest in. We were handed a list of 19 items that Willie Watt, Kamal Hanna (Director of Finance), and Eileen Klinkig (Assistant to the Director of Finance) consider when selecting stocks. The list includes factors such as the earnings records for at least the last five years of a company's activities, the gross revenue of the company, the industry in which the company falls (i.e. is it cyclical, somewhat recession proof, etc.), reports from financial analysts, and world wide events. The stocks Makivik has purchased over the years have all met these criteria.

Our investment strategy is not risky. For example, Makivik only buys stocks in Canadian companies that have sales of more than $200 million per year. We currently have shares in 23 Canadian companies in the stock portfolio. Among them are 5 banks, 3 oil companies, a smattering of

transportation and communication stocks, mines, electronics, and food companies. One of the best performing stocks in our Canadian section is Northern Telecom. A snapshot of the portfolio taken on April 30th, 1992 shows that the average cost for our 1,500 Northern Telecom shares was $23.65 per share. The market price on that day was $48.50 per share, more than double what we paid for it. Not all the results are that good, of course. But the overall result among the 23 Canadian stocks is positive. The total cost of our Canadian stocks at April 30th, 1992 was $835,507, versus a market value of $847,397. That's not counting the dividends the companies pay to Makivik, as a shareholder of their stocks.

The stock portfolio also has 75 US stocks. Makivik buys stocks in US companies that have annual sales of over $1 billion. We asked why there were so many US stocks. It's because there are more US companies which meet our investment criteria in the US than in Canada.

Makivik held, for example, 1000 shares of Coca-Cola for $55.74 (US), and it was worth $83 (US) per share on April 30th, 1992. Among the well known US stocks in the portfolio are: American Express, Campbell Soup, Walt Disney, Kodak, Heinz, IBM, Kellogg, Quaker Oats, and Westinghouse Electric. All are well known name brands, all with annual sales of more than $1 billion. Very secure blue chip stocks. The US stocks were bought for $5,675,875 (Cdn), and were worth $6,245,118 (Cdn) on April 30th, 1992.

The stock prices are constantly monitored by Makivik's

Finance Department. About ten stock market transactions are made each week. On the morning we inquired, Eileen Klinkig was busy looking over the quarterly earnings for Bristol Meyers (a US pharmaceutical company). The profits came out much lower than expected. The stock fell by six dollars as a result, and she viewed it as an opportunity to buy.

Gazing down the list of factors to consider when selecting stocks, we asked about #19: worldwide events (economic, politics etc.). Last year's war in the Persian Gulf is a good example. Klinkig says, "Everyone expected the stock market to fall quite dramatically when war broke out. However within a matter of days it was clear the war would not last that long. It was a very short drop and then it came back much more strongly than it was before." Makivik, of course, purchased stocks during the low period.

We asked about the recent Olympia and York real estate crisis, which could mean millions in losses for Canadian banks (Makivik owns stock in the five biggest). The bank stocks have dipped below their 52 week lows, and Makivik is following them very closely to take advantage of opportunities to purchase some of the stock.

Currently there is roughly $6.5 million invested in the stock market. At a recent Makivik Board of Directors meeting in March 1992, a decision was taken to increase the amount in the stock market up to $20 million. Klinkig says this will be done gradually, as stocks become attractive to buy. The investment criteria won't change. It will mean buying more shares of Coca-Cola, for example, rather than

finding new, perhaps riskier companies to invest in.

The capital to invest in the stock market will be shifted from the money market (short-term) portfolio. This is where the bulk of the Initial and JBNQA Implementation Fund is invested. Approximately $71 million are invested in the money markets. Short term deposits and short-term notes are basically anything maturing up to one year. Canada and Provincial Treasury Bills are examples of short term deposits. Before interest rates went down. Makivik was getting over 10% return on the money market investments. Now that interest rates are hovering at around 6%, the yield on our short term deposits is between 6.25% and 6.5%. Between October 1991 and March 1992, the yield was roughly 8%.

Makivik also has over $5.5 million invested in the bond market, again with very conservative investment criteria (no junk bonds). They are mostly mid to long term marketable bonds (5 to 20 year maturity dates from time of purchase). Makivik owns bonds issued by the Government of Canada, and some crown corporations, such as Ontario Hydro, and Hydro-Québec. We also have some corporate bonds issued by Bell Canada Enterprises, Trans-Canada Pipeline, and Imasco among others. The yield on Makivik's bond portfolio in the fiscal year of 1990-1991 for example was 11.4%.

Typically, when one thinks of the money markets, one thinks of someone stuck on the phone all day long. We asked if the people who make the investments spend their time like that. Not really. The people in the Finance Department who handle the portfolio investments spend much of their time reading. The business section of *The Globe and Mail, The Financial Post*, and the *Wall Street Journal* are read daily. The Finance Department also subscribes to some specialized financial reports. Then, for the stock portfolio they read the annual and quarterly reports of all the companies they invest in, as well as broker reports *Standard and Poors,* and *Value Line*.

So when it comes time to make investment decisions, they are well informed. When they do get on the phone with the broker to invest, it happens very fast. Money market has to be done within a matter of minutes, for example. In general, the best time to invest is between 8:30 and 9:30 in the morning, when the product is still there on the market. You have to be able to make snap decisions.

We asked Eileen Klinkig how she felt about investing the heritage fund of the Inuit of Nunavik. Klinkig, who made her first trip to Nunavik for the AGM last March, thought for a second. "There's a certain responsibility towards it," she began. "You're sitting in a very unique situation. I'm not investing for a company where if you lose a million dollars of their capital, they can recover it through increasing the price of goods sold, or cut down on costs elsewhere. The opportunity to make back the capital that you might lose is not there. So we have to be very careful and protect the capital, protect the heritage fund for the future."

With that in mind, we asked how the 1987 stock market crash affected the people working on the portfolio. Kamal

Hanna, the Director of Finance remembers, "It was very difficult to gauge what was going to happen in the stock market. What we did was we went in and we started purchasing the stocks at the lower rate. We would buy and sell frequently, sometimes buying a stock in the morning and selling in the afternoon. I think what we did in the end by taking advantage of the market fluctuations after the stock market crashed proved to be beneficial to the corporation."

Indeed it has. Willie Watt, who was first elected Treasurer when Makivik was created, and has been reelected since, has seen the investments in stocks, bonds, and the money market grow tremendously over the years. With the recent decision to increase the stock portfolio to $20 million, Watt will undoubtedly see more growth in the "Nunavik Heritage Fund" in the years ahead.

(Makivik News, Summer 1992, page 19)

Seaku's Scallops in Salluit: Developing a Fishery for Local Markets and Beyond...

Surusiluk Keataınak is one of Nunavik's "new entrepreneurs." He's 45 years old with a wife and five children. He lives in Salluit where he was born and is presently hoping to develop a small scale business harvesting scallops from Hudson Strait waters. He wants to sell his catches in Salluit and nearby communities. He has had some limited success in selling his catches at $10 a pound to nearby communities.

In 1986 he purchased a $27,000 three year old trawler from Newfoundland with the assistance of another Inuk and money from the Inuit Loan Fund. Ever since that time he has been active in using his boat taking researchers out to the various waters off Nunavik. He has since bought his partner out and is now sole owner of the vessel.

In those early years, Makivik Corporation's Research Department (today called the Renewable Resources Department) was the only researcher of Nunavik's coastal waters. They eventually involved the Kativik Regional Government (KRG), the federal Department of Fisheries and Oceans (DFO), and later on, Seaku Fisheries (a Makivik subsidiary). Key people from Makivik's Renewable Resource Department were transferred to Seaku, and Seaku was then mandated to identify and develop marine resources exhibiting commercial potential. Seaku is under

the direction of Jackie Koneak, Second Vice-President of Makivik Corporation, and President of Seaku Fisheries Incorporated.

Keatainak and his vessel have not been the only operation that has participated in such research in the past few years. Boats from Quaqtaq, Kangiqsualuujjuaq and Kuujjuaq have also been used for such studies. At present, Bob Deer of Quaqtaq is also developing a scallop fishery in the Diana Bay region.

During the first year of research in waters between Quaqtaq and Salluit they used scallop drags, also known as "Digby drags" to collect the bottom dwelling creatures. Since concentrations of scallops looked promising between those communities they reasoned that they should also check out nearby waters. The next summer they explored the coastal waters between Salluit to just south of Inukjuak. Although present, they found that there were less significant concentrations of scallops in the Hudson Bay waters.

Marc Allard of Seaku Fisheries said that based on research and commercial test fishing, the best areas for harvesting scallops tended to be in depths of between 20 and 40 fathoms. He added that, "although scallop research began in 1983, a research project that coincided with the 1987 Elders Conference in Quaqtaq caused a flurry of excitement, and created a demand for scallop products. Inuit knew that scallops existed as the odd storm would wash empty shells ashore, but they never had the means to harvest them. Anyway, as we were conducting research in the area at the time, and having caught a few scallops we decided to drop them off in town. We gave them away at that time since our permit did not allow us to sell our catches and was only for research purposes. They were very well received and appreciated by the community and delegates."

With more research, Seaku Fisheries determined that there was a good possibility that a small scallop operation could make a viable commercial operation in the Hudson Strait area. Last summer Keatainak and Seaku began a two year program to fully assess the commercial potential of this resource. The first year was to identify areas with good scallop concentrations. This summer they will be researching the harvesting, processing, and market possibilities to find out how and where it would be best to sell small commercial catches. Seaku and Keatainak also want to know what demand exists for various scallop products (fresh or frozen meats, or whole scallops), and set up a distribution network.

Seaku's Allard says, "It's unlikely that there will be a large scale commercial fishery in Nunavik waters as there is in southern Canada. The Nunavik market can only absorb product from a few boats. We have seen from our surveys that only small commercial operations could be supported on a regional level, such as through inter-community trade."

Allard continues, "The idea is to eventually develop sustainable and viable scallop fisheries. No scallop harvesting operation can fully go commercial until we are sure that future generations can benefit from this renewable

resource. Furthermore, any commercial development that arises from Nunavik waters will not be able to compete with the southern commercial fisheries. For one thing, long established fisheries from the maritime provinces are able to sell their catches at substantially lower prices. This is because they have lower maintenance and operating costs over a much longer season, and have all the marine infra-structures necessary to support their commercial activities. The Nunavik region is hampered by the lack of infrastruc-ture such as wharves and processing and freezing facilities."

It is not easy having to maintain a vessel for purposes of northern commercial fishing. Keatainak has had to buy a new engine for his boat through the local co-op, which cost about $15,000. He says, "Actually it was a good price, but it goes to show that the original price for the purchase of any boat is always an initial cost, since money is con-stantly needed to maintain such investments, such as for upkeep and payment of employees working for me."

"However, I found that it is possible to make a small profit selling the scallops I harvested, to communities close to Salluit. I have to emphasize that I cannot make large profits from what I have now, since the boat has a lim-ited holding capacity, we had to contend with bad sum-mer weather like last year and Nunavik has a short marine season to begin with." Keatainak can make a small profit on his scallops because he can sell directly to the consumer, cutting out the costly middlemen.

His operation will eventually be regulated by the De-partment of Fisheries and Oceans (DFO), which has been providing him with an exploratory permit to carry out the research in conjunction with Seaku. Although there is currently little competition, Keatainak says, "Any scallop harvesting activity will have to be very well monitored and regulated. There has been some significant research, yet more studies are needed to find out the true extent of the resource in the Hudson Strait waters. We all have to make sure that the scallops that we have are not fished out right away, and ascertain at what level we can harvest them, so that future generations can benefit from this natural renewable resource."

(Makivik News, Summer 1992, page 33)

Freezers! Building Inter-Community Trade

Blueprints, tools, heavy equipment, construction workers, plans. All are elements of the project known as Inter-Community Trade. With the construction of 3 freezers this summer, we're witnessing the start of something big.

Makivik Corporation is developing a uniquely northern commercial and employment initiative that will benefit Nunavik on local and regional levels. The objective is to create jobs for middle aged Inuit men (45-65 years of age) who are still skilled in the traditional activities of hunting, fishing and trapping. They will harvest the natural wildlife resources which will be sold initially within Nunavik through an inter-community trade system.

This particular age group, since the 1960s, has been generally left out of the job market, being unilingual. Though they are extremely skilled in their traditional activities and even highly respected and envied for their free lifestyle, they have always found it difficult to maintain their livelihoods.

Their economic standing has always been easily affected by southern moods and changing attitudes. One has only to look back at the decline of fox fur and mature seal pelt market prices (the legacy of Greenpeace). Furthermore, Nunavik Inuit are restricted by Québec laws that forbid the selling of wild meat. Such laws are being amended, as is the JBNQA. The change to the Agreement will be such that subsistence activities of Nunavik Inuit will still be protected.

New Freezers

Makivik is pleased to announce that modern handling facilities (measuring 50 x 30 x 18 feet) costing approxi mately $450,000 each, were constructed in the three communities of Umiujaq, Quaqtaq and Kangiqsualujjuaq this summer. Bruno Pilozzi, Makivik's financial adviser says, "This is an initiative using Makivik's money, and presently we are in the process of making funding applications to the federal government for them to help provide the needed facilities for all Nunavik communities."

Construction of the handling facilities ended in late September, except for Quaqtaq, which is expected to continue until mid-October. Honco Incorporated built the three large buildings. Their location was determined by proximity to water, power, and the condition of the soil. All three were built on solid bedrock, and have cement bases. The interior is a special fiberglass material approved for slaughterhouse use. Inside, there are two sections, physically divided by a wall. This is because the facilities will handle fish, and meats, which cannot be in the same room in order to comply with government regulations. Soon, work tables, cutting tools, shrink wrappers, small blast freezers and other equipment will arrive to fill the buildings.

The handling facilities will be used to prepare raw products for shipment to the regional slaughterhouses. For example, if a community harvests caribou, the animals will be gutted, quartered, skinned, and packed for transport to

the slaughterhouse, where they would be inspected, processed, and packaged, (just like southern meats) for Nunavik consumers. The slaughterhouses will likely be constructed during the summer of 1993. There has been no final decision regarding the communities where the three slaughterhouses will be built. They are expected to cost roughly $3 million each.

The summer of 1993 will also see the construction of more handling facilities in other communities. Eventually, all Nunavik communities will have one. They will all be able to do refined cutting of meats for local consumption. Makivik will establish a new subsidiary company to manage the meat processing and marketing aspect of Inter-Community Trade.

Choosing the Resource

The initial plan is to mandate local Hunting, Fishing and Trapping Associations to identify their particular wildlife resource concentrations and ascertain which species they will be able to harvest on a sustainable level. Examples can include caribou meat from Kuujjuaq, arctic char from Kangiqsualujjuaq and Tasiujaq, seal meat from Kangiqsujuaq, scallops from Quaqtaq and Salluit, ptarmigans from Umiujaq and so on. All communities are expected to be able to contribute the wildlife products that their particular region can produce.

This will make it possible for communities to have available a variety of northern meat products. Some communities, for example, cannot harvest seals year round. Furthermore, not all regions have scallops either, as mentioned in our last issue of *Makivik News (see page 87).* Therefore, a system that can provide such unavailable foodstuff will improve the nutritional dietary balance of the Inuit. Incidentally, arctic char will only be commercialized on a limited basis, being already used for subsistence and commercial activities (mainly fishing camps, and fisheries that are already operating).

In keeping with past philosophy and wildlife management principles, subsistence activities will be the priority, meaning that commercial activities will not dominate the usual hunting, trapping and fishing activities of the Inuit population. Inter-community trading will only be able to harvest wildlife resources after making certain that local needs will not be compromised.

As mentioned, Makivik is in the initial planning stage to establish a five year funding arrangement with the governments to establish infrastructures in all the communities and to meet operating costs. Hunters and fishermen also have to be assured that there will be enough money to fund the buying of their catches. It is important for them to know that the system will be able to provide a predictable level of income so that they may be able to plan their efforts and assure them that such revenue will not depend on market fluctuations. A promise of guaranteed income is necessary to create a sense of security and cement long term planning and personal commitments.

The Associations will be the ones establishing zones and finalizing quotas for the various seasons. The inter-com-

munity trade organization envisaged will be responsible for maintaining the quality of the wild meat and shipment to the processing facilities.

Training will be needed to teach people to use the new equipment and familiarize them with the handling facilities. Such training programs will start in the near future, once the infrastructures are available.

The catches would then be sold to local people in the communities. Though such sale to local markets should not be expected to be immediately financially viable, the planned selling of northern produce to southern markets should eventually prove profitable.

The present Hunter Support programs—already well established in the communities—will continue their harvesting for local people who are unable to hunt and fish on their own. In fact, with commercialization, a much clearer clarification and definition of roles between inter community trade and the Hunter Support program will become possible.

Then...and Now

The fur trade played a major part in the history of Canadian native peoples, since it drew upon a very skilled group of trappers. But this flourishing trade, as we all know, was destroyed recently by special interest groups. Secondly, there was the creation of the soapstone carving economy in the 1950s and 60s. Again, it drew upon a skill inherent in many Inuit. However, they were dependent on southern markets, which dictated the prices of their furs and carvings.

Inter-community trade is slightly different in that the initiative is brought about by Inuit themselves—in this case, Makıvık Corporation. They will build the necessary handling, processing and inspection infrastructures, set up a network that will buy the wildlife products that the hunters, trappers and fishermen harvest, and will develop the northern and southern markets. And, who knows, perhaps we will establish trading posts in Great Britain.

(Makivik News, Fall 1992, page 7)

Landholding Corporations: On Solid Ground

From raising money to raising awareness, Nunavik Landholding Corporations (LHCs) have changed tremendously over the life of the James Bay and Northern Québec Agreement (JBNQA). In past years, LHCs have been almost totally dependent upon grants for their operations. In fact, financing has always been a main problem for Landholdings. Once, many referred to LHCs as the "poor child" of the JBNQA. While their existence is central to the JBNQA and financing was provided for other organizations in the Agreement, Landholding Corporations received no provision for ongoing funding. They work to finance themselves from the administration of Category I lands. The direct funding that Makivik used to provide for LHCs in past years was discontinued due to budget constraints. Through the growing pains of establishing proper organizational and financial management strategies, in time many Landholding subsidiaries have come to fruition and certain Landholding Corporations are not only becoming more and more self-supportive, but they are also able to support other interests in the communities.

As owners of Category I lands, LHCs can grant leases and occupation permits to individuals and businesses and can collect money from these grants. Lots that are used for public services, such as government funded schools, clinics, and police stations, are charged an annual token sum of $1.

Land leases that are granted for more than five years need to have the consent of the members. The members are the beneficiaries of the community that the LHC represents. The Québec government, however, still holds the mining and subsurface rights to Category I lands, with the exception of soapstone. Landholding Corporations must approve any mining activity and be compensated for it. Gravel used for such things as road fill is legally considered "minerals," so LHCs receive compensation for access to gravel quarries.

The Nayumivik LHC of Kuujjuaq, with the largest population in the region, plays a key role in the development of the community, which is becoming a veritable metropolitan site compared to most other Nunavik communities. Nayumivik was a signatory of the Kuujjuaq Agreement (1998), which provided $48.5 million in compensation for the diversion of the Caniapiscau River. Nayumivik President Willie Gordon explained that the success of their LHC has allowed Nayumivik to contribute major amounts to the community in donations over the 1994 fiscal year. This included $100,000 towards Kuujjuaq's new bowling lanes, $200,000 in "gas rebates" which was dispensed equally to beneficiary households, around $40,000 for the women's shelter, and funding towards other activities and festivals.

The Nayumivik LHC recuperated $19,000 from the sale of old metal barrels that were collected from nearby abandoned sites. Other community projects that Nayumivik directors have planned are the purchase of Global Po-

sitioning Systems and a marine mapping project for boating navigation, a trail upgrading project, and a community public carpentry shop. They are also providing special long-term land leases so that residents who are participating in the new home ownership program can acquire mortgages. Willie Gordon mentions, "I personally would like to thank Makivik Corporation for the annual budgets that we have received to get us prepared. Now, we are doing the best we can and we are doing very well."

Landholdings have always been identified by Makivik and the Kativik Regional Development Corporation (KRDC) as very important players in the field of economic development. LHCs have a representative who sits on the Board of Directors of KRDC along with other Nunavik organizations. LHC development usually progresses according to the extent that LHCs are proactive, the size of the community, and the size of local development projects. Now in Salluit for example, the Qarqalik LHC, and the Nunaturlik LHC of Kangiqsujjuaq are planning subsidiary ventures for when the Raglan mining project gets under way. They have also created local advisory committees to decide upon the wisest plans for distributing compensation funds.

A common goal of Landholding Corporations is to create employment for their respective residents. In the summer of 1993, the Nunaturlik LHC created Ammuumaajuq Adventures with that very goal in mind for the Inuit of Kangiqsujjuaq. Ammuumaajuq is working to turn the area into a popular, and successful, tourist destination—one of their most popular attractions being the crater Pingualuit.

In legal terms, LHCs were incorporated by the effect of a section in the Respecting Land Regime in the James Bay and New Québec Territories, a specific provision in the James Bay and Northern Québec Agreement (JBNQA). In the Agreement, they are identified as "Inuit Community Corporations." In July 1994, Makivik's Legal Department updated and fine-tuned past LHC guidelines, including all aspects of these "nonprofit associations," as an important tool for each LHC in the form of an "Instruction Manual for Landholding Corporations." The Manual explains that LHCs cannot invest in projects that will benefit only a few individuals. LHC profits are used for the benefit of the whole community.

One very important duty of LHCs is to maintain the beneficiary lists. Each LHC receives $735 plus $1 per beneficiary from the Québec Ministry of Health and Social Services for keeping a track of their list of beneficiaries.

Still fitting, perhaps, the description of the "poor child" are the LHCs in some of the smaller communities. Martha Kauki, President of Kangirsuk's Saputik Landholding Corporation says, "We have had a shortage of funding ever since I have been with Saputik (four years ago)." A construction company is planning to continue some renovations to the school in that community this summer. Although the land occupied by the government funded school brings in a token amount per year to the LHC, while the construction is taking place, there is a chance to gain revenues through the sale of gravel and temporary

land leasing to the contractors. Construction projects, especially in the smaller communities, are not always ongoing. A big year in rental income may be followed by a very small year. In Kangirsuk, as partial payment to the LHC, the construction company agrees to do some maintenance on the Saputik owned office building.

One important responsibility that LHCs have taken action upon is environmental cleanliness. Printed out of big rocks in parking-space-sized capital letters on a level rise of tundra across the Arnaud River from Kangirsuk are the words: "OCEANIC PAYNE BAY." The landmark was placed there to signal aircraft to the location of an iron ore find in the early fifties. The only thing that moved in the area while *Makivik News* visited the site are two ptarmigan and the radiator fan of a rusted John Deere tractor that has been spinning in the breeze for about forty years.

Good bearings

For those with a curiosity for 1950s mining technology, the site may be an interesting find, but for Martha Kauki, and Saputik Director Willie Thomassie, it is an eyesore that must be taken care of. The local area and shoreline is strewn with a variety of old domestic junk, rusted barrels (many full), propane tanks, and large metal parts identifiable to mining engineers. A clean-up project for the site that was first planned by the local Municipal Corporation of Kangirsuk has been handed over to Saputik. The LHC is attempting to get funding from government departments that are responsible for environmental clean-ups. including a percentage to manage the project.

In Kuujjuaraapik a commercial venture is being planned that will benefit Inuit residents there. Present owners of the Auberge Sinittavik Lodge may join with a subsidiary of Sakkuq LHC to expand the existing hotel. Naturally, with plans for the Great Whale Project resting on ice, there will not be a need for as many rooms as it was first thought. Unique to Sakkuq, the Landholding Corporation covers both the communities of Kuujjuaraapik and Umiujaq, although they each have separate Boards. This situation stems from a past idea, when it was thought that the full Inuit population from Kuujjuaraapik would move to the new community of Umiujaq.

Makivik News asked Stephen Grasser, the KRDC Development Officer based in Salluit, about the various LHCs working relationships with each other. He explains that, although there is no framework for regular meetings among the various Landholding Corporations, the idea of creating a regional Landholding body has been discussed. "Certainly all LHCs can learn from each others' success and failures," Grasser says. After the success of Kuujjuaq, Willie Gordon is very willing to help other communities. "For example, even if it is a small community, funds can be generated. Even old barrels are worth money. There may be ways for other communities to make money that they may not know about," he says.

Grasser has worked on files for LHCs from Kangirsuk to Akulivik since 1989. "There are many good news stories coming out of these communities," he says. These

stories include the news of three subsidiary companies which belong to the Tuvaaluk Landholding Corporation in Quaqtaq: Ikkaruq Service Center which deals in small engine vehicles and hunting supplies; Kuvviti Fuel Inc., which owns fuel storage tanks and provides heating fuel and gasoline in Quaqtaq; and Annisaq Leasing, which owns and rents office space to various organizations. Bob Deer, manager for Tuvaaluk, says that when he first became involved with Landholding about twelve years ago, there was a big need for proper organization. "Today, we realize that unless we have trained personnel or sufficient plans with proper direction, the Landholdings will have difficulty in developing. Especially since they represent the communities and they play a very important role in development."

Peter Inukpuk is the Manager of Inukjuak's Pituvik LHC. He explains, "We Inuit have lived for (thousands of years) as truly free people. We do not (fully) have the concept of land ownership in our culture. While people in other parts of the world were collecting thrones, we were protected by the cold." He adds, "We had better adopt that concept if we plan to stay in the game."

Besides owning Category I lands, LHCs also have some responsibilities regarding access to category I and II lands for sport hunting and fishing. Although category II lands are owned by the Québec government, LHCs must authorize all outfitting permits and commercial hunting and fishing licenses for these activities on the lands. This applies to both natives and non-natives. All new camps are controlled by Inuit and non-native partners own no more than

49% of shares in them. Natives have the exclusive right to hunt and fish in Category I and II lands, while non-natives must meet the conditions established by LHCs, including quotas and the purchase of special hunting and fishing permits. "We can issue licenses and set quotas, but (due to a lack of resources) we have no conservation officers. Therefore we cannot execute the rules that we set," Peter Inukpuk explains. He feels that this will become a more important matter to be taken on if certain species are significantly reduced. Inukpuk believes that there are three stages that communities go through in recognizing their full authority: "There are communities that are not completely sure they own the land, then there are communities which 'think' they own the land, and finally there are feelings and actions that, 'yes', we do own the land," he says. "Whether we stay with Québec or separate, we still have to deal with land. No matter what flag the community is flying. We cannot afford to be unorganized about land management. If we are not able to organize our own land someone else will do it. But that means we will be less of an owner than they are," Peter Inukpuk says. "We want to find solutions that will benefit Inuit." When asked about the work that Pituvik, like other Landholding Corporations assume to maintain a uncontaminated territory, he says that one day, Inuit in Nunavik will truly feel and know they own the land, and "it will be with pride. The land cannot dirty itself. People dirty the land, so it is the people that have to keep it clean." As Nunavik communities, with assistance from their Landholding Corporations, continue to benefit from the beauty of their environment, it appears they will also be enjoying more profits from the development of that environment as well.

(Makivik News, Summer 1995, page 5)

Sammy Kudluk

A Star is Born

Nunavik Arctic Foods was the "toast of the town" on May 1st at a press conference to officially launch the company to the southern public. Held at the Institut du tourisme et d'hôtellerie du Québec (ITHQ)—Montréal's renowned cooking school—the main speaker was Mark T. Gordon, president of NAF. "It is with great pride" he stated in his opening speech, "that we are standing before you today launching a new company that will generate revenue for the Inuit and make available a unique product in the south." Also sharing the spotlight were Marcel Landry, the Québec minister of agriculture, fisheries and food (MAPAQ) and David Cliche, Québec deputy parliamentary assistant for native affairs. Minister Landry welcomed Nunavik Arctic Foods into the Québec food industry and to mark this achievement, presented Mark T. Gordon with four MAPAQ permits. These will allow the inspected meat from the processing plants to be sold outside Nunavik throughout Québec. Michel Guygère and Chef Jean-Paul Grappe of ITHQ also took the podium and spoke about the tremendous opportunities such country food enterprises offer the culinary world. Mr. Grappe said it was a great day for chefs everywhere, proclaiming caribou "the king of game animals" due to its high protein, low fat and natural tenderness. Bruno Pilozzi, Economic Development Department Head, acted as moderator for the event and fielded questions from the attending journalists. The press coverage which appeared during the week of the conference was extremely positive and plentiful. Fifteen (and still counting!) radio, television and newspaper stories appeared, which included a front page feature story in *The Gazette* Business Section. Also present at the launch were the Makivik executives, Ambassador Mary Simon, NAF staff and numerous provincial and federal government representatives. The May 1st event was in succession to the northern press opportunity which took place at the Makivik AGM held in March. Nunavik Arctic Foods next challenge—filling the endless requests for caribou products generated by all the attention!

(Makivik News, Summer 1995, page 44)

Ipushin: Potential on the Hoof
By Bob Mesher

A gigantic boulder lies buried beneath the sand near the west wall of Inukjuak's old weather station. The rock is large, but it was not too big of an obstacle to be overcome by the construction crew who renovated the building last fall into a processing plant for the Ipushin International Trading Company (IITC). Blasting the boulder out of the way would have disturbed the foundation of the existing infrastructure. So, instead of having the ramp for transport trucks positioned straight into the plant, it was decided to change the blueprints so that trucks can now back in on an angle and to one side of the hidden boulder. The rock was not the first, nor will it likely be the last obstacle that Ipushin will have to deal with.

The word "Ipushin" is derived from the family names of the President and the Vice-President of the new company—Mr. Jobie Epoo and Mr. Dongshuk Shin. Inukjuak's Caripoo Trading Company, (which has been dealing in caribou "hard horns" since 1991) and a Korean company based in Los Angeles called Zion Enterprise Inc. have jointly created the new caribou harvesting operation, now possible following changes to the Province of Québec's Wildlife Act (Bill #12) which was passed June 17, 1994.

Jobie Epoo is enthusiastic about Ipushin as he describes what will be involved in the major operation. "We are going to be herding caribou into near Inukjuak, releasing

those that are not accepted by Agriculture Canada, and slaughtering up to 100 per day. The caribou carcasses will be cut in halves and transported by Ipushin trucks to the processing plant in the community where they will be processed and packaged for sale," he told *Makivik News* late last fall.

Ipushin's business plan describes a two-phase project to be carried out over the next five years. Phase one includes "research in caribou biology and behavior for the purposes of assessing the economic feasibility of husbandry, experimenting with herding techniques, meeting government inspection standards, establishing a predictable level of production, and streamlining the different processes involved at the industrial and commercial levels of this project."

The second phase, which would begin in the third year of operation, will include "implementing the process on a professional scale as well as developing a number of caribou husbandry projects in the communities that use the Leaf River herd."

Besides holding a quota to slaughter 3,000 head of caribou over a seven month period, IITC also has a permit to hold 110 head of caribou in captivity for research purposes starting in the spring of 1996. The purpose of their research project will be to study how the caribou react to being controlled by herders, to gather nutritional information about the animals, and generally to find an efficient way of developing domesticated caribou herds in Nunavik which can sustain commercial projects. It is in the best interest of Ipushin, as a commercial venture, to preserve and understand the caribou—their primary resource. Past studies have shown that it is possible for caribou to adapt to captivity, but to what extent has yet to be proven.

Quotas are reviewed by the government annually, and Ipushin hopes to be allowed to slaughter 5,000 head the first year, and then doubling its quota annually until a maximum of 50,000 head per year is reached. Jobie Epoo points out that if Ipushin were to operate at a peak efficiency, the caribou population could still sustain other commercial ventures.

Makivik Corporation has committed an investment of $200,000 in IITC. Ipushin first had to show proof of approval from government departments such as a quota permit from the environmental section of the Ministère de l'Environnement et de la Faune (MEF), and approval from Agriculture Canada. Ipushin has also agreed to assist and collaborate with the operations of Nunavik Arctic Foods. During a Makivik Board of Directors meeting in November, it was agreed by both Ipushin and Makivik to accept the appointment of Peter Adams, as a representative for Makivik, on Ipushin's Board of Directors. Peter is entitled to vote at Ipushin meetings and enjoy the same rights as the other Ipushin BOD members.

According to research conducted prior to writing the Ipushin Business Plan, the George River caribou herd is estimated to have around 800,000 head and the Leaf River herd has about 260,000 head. Scientific studies and Inuit knowledge also suggest that these herds are growing at such a rate that we can expect that the caribou can eat

themselves out of existence. Culling large numbers of animals out of the Leaf River herd, according to this information, should only improve the herd's chances of continued survival.

Jobie Epoo explains the reasons for selecting the Leaf River herd rather than from the George River herd. "For me to make a request to harvest caribou from the George River herd would have involved going to many more government offices and Native groups. It is simpler for me to harvest caribou from only the Leaf River herd," he says.

It is also the only caribou herd that migrates into the area of Inukjuak. "Our herders are most likely going to be from Inukjuak, Puvirnituq, Umiujaq, and Akulivik," he says. A major consideration for IITC is that they must take care not to upset the traditional subsistence hunt as well. Their business plan also states, "this project can be profitable for all communities that share the Leaf River herd and Ipushin welcomes shared ownership of the business."

While construction workers were busy completing the renovations for the processing plant, another crew were drilling holes for 2,500 fence posts near Inukjuak. Five feet high plastic fencing will be supported on the posts, topped by burlap which will prevent the caribou from seeing beyond and thus stampeding. Holding live caribou in captivity ensures selection, allows the animals to be inspected, and also makes it possible to plan production.

Caribou will be tunneled through extended fences into a large holding yard with a capacity of 3,000 animals. From there, 500 can be selected and held in three holding pens for each week's processing. Ipushin must provide feed for any animals that are held for more than 48 hours, and corrals and pens have to be cleaned after each group of animals. A stock of hay, "hay pellets" (a condensed nutrition product), and wood chips will have to be stored near the corral site.

Those caribou which meet Agriculture Canada inspection standards will be channeled into a mobile slaughterhouse. From there, the carcasses are stored in refrigerated trucks and brought to the processing plant in Inukjuak. The meat will then be packed and shipped south for distribution. While Québec is the largest and closest market for caribou, IITC has learned that the meat is also desirable in other countries.

Makivik News asked Mr. Epoo how they plan to keep track of animals out on the land. "There are about nine caribou in the Leaf River herd that have been collared by the Québec government and are monitored by satellite. All we need to do is ask for their location," he explains. He says that in winter, herders will use snowmobiles to control the caribou and in the summer, helicopters.

Jobie also considers traditional herding methods, which have been proven to work well on different terrain and livestock in other parts of the world as possible methods of corralling Leaf River caribou. "I am studying horses," he says. "It's going to be an approach that I seriously will be looking at—bringing maybe six or seven horses to Inukjuak. Four wheelers can't travel very fast, track trucks in the summer are not very good, and helicopters are very ex-

pensive. So on foot with sheep dogs and horses are something of great interest to me," he says. He explains that while Ipushin will have their own full-time herders, anybody from neighboring communities who want to form a herding crew will be paid so much per head for each caribou that they round up. Herding will take place year round except for mating season which takes place throughout October. Female caribou will be spared between April and September.

Interest in caribou herding grew out of the Caripoo Trading Company's sale of "hard horns" to a Korean Company based in Los Angeles, and by-product sales continue to be a major component of the Ipushin caribou herding venture. The antler business was successful from its very beginning in 1991. "Hard horns" are antlers which have fallen to the ground during the shedding season. Prices for all caribou parts are subject to fluctuation, and hard horns fetch about $6 per pound. Antlers which are taken during the first 55 days of growth (which is early summer for female caribou and late summer for males) are worth substantially more than other caribou parts which makes the collection of these new growth antlers a very attractive venture for all parties.

Jobie explains, "A few years ago I made a proposal to the government to fence in caribou, de-horn them, and release them. They said, 'No way can you do that!' Then I had to think of another plan, so I tried buying hard horns from local gatherers," he says. Although dehorning businesses are operating in other parts of the world, this practice is not allowed in Québec. During the months that caribou begin to grow new antlers, though, at Ipushin it will be business as usual and they will be able to take a certain quantity of the more valuable horns along with the meat and other by-products.

Other parts such as sinews, penises, and skins, will be sold as by-products of the Ipushin operation which is based mainly on the sale of caribou meat. "The only thing that we have not had a buyer for yet is the viscera," says Jobie. A designated area will be fenced in to contain waste products from the operation, such as the guts, some skins, and some bones. There will be spread for composting on a five-year trail basis, along with the ashes of any contaminated animals. Their business plan points out Ipushin is seeking the expertise of Agriculture Canada and environmental authorities in order to make the composting operation a success. The location of the site will be chosen with water contamination as well as odorous and visual pollution in mind.

The new IITC project can potentially accommodate some positive spin-offs such as providing services to existing Inter-Community Trade operations, job creation in many areas of expertise ranging from helicopter pilots to butchers in a region with very high unemployment. Ipushin also talks of the possibility of integrating caribou management into a college curriculum for Nunavik.

The thing that seems most certain though, as the Ipushin documentation states, "Whether it be for caribou meat or by-products, the demand far exceeds the supply."

For the time being, that eliminates one more obstacle in the way of success for the new Ipushin Intercontinental Trading Company.

(Makivik News, Winter 1995/1996, page 20)

Bob Mesher

Seaku: Ten Years of Shrimp Fishing
By Stephen Hendrie

On July 24, 1996 Makivik's subsidiary company, Seaku Fisheries Incorporated, will celebrate its tenth anniversary. In ten years, the company's activities have helped employ over 100 Inuit fishermen from the Nunavik region and has developed a model fishery that is attracting attention from indigenous groups as far away as Nicaragua.

There is plenty to be told about Seaku. Its main area of activity is the management of Makivik's offshore shrimp fishing license, which includes participating in the selection and training of Inuit fishermen together with Unaaq Fisheries (which it owns in a 50% joint venture partnership with Qiqiktaaluk Corporation in Nunavut). Seaku has also conducted numerous research and development projects in Nunavik's coastal waters aimed at identifying and developing viable and sustainable community based fishing operations with Inuit entrepreneurs. It is now contemplating getting into the field of International Development. In this first installment, we will take a look at its mainstay, the operation of the offshore shrimp fishery.

Jackie Koneak, Makivik's Second Vice-President, Seaku Fisheries President and also Unaaq's President is happy about the work Seaku has accomplished over the past ten years. He acknowledges, however, that at this point it is getting harder and harder, like most fisheries, to make a buck. Koneak points to the fact that in 1996 the Department of

Fisheries and Oceans will slap a minimum $130,000 access fee on the holders of offshore shrimp fishing licenses. There are three of these licenses that are currently being exploited by Inuit from Nunavik and Nunavut. One is held by Seaku, another is held by Qiqiktaaluk Corporation from Baffin Island and the third license is held jointly by Seaku and Qiqiktaaluk and managed by Unaaq. These new fees will clearly dig into the profits of the Inuit license holders as well as the operators of the boats who fish these licenses for the Inuit companies. The beauty of the Seaku operation is that there is little risk involved. Makivik learned with its first fishing venture, Imaqpik Fisheries, that holding both the license and operating the boat was a highly risky operation. The result was that Makivik lost money in the operation, closed it down, but held on to the license. The license lay dormant for a few years and then was fished under "royalty charter" for a few years whereby shrimp fishing vessels were chartered to harvest the shrimp allocation and share the profits with the Inuit license holder. In 1986 Farocan entered the picture. Farocan knew that Seaku had a shrimp license but no vessel to fish it so they proposed to build and operate the required vessel if Seaku would enter into a long term agreement allowing them to fish our shrimp allocation. Put the two companies together and you have the makings of a fishing marriage made in heaven. The essential part of the deal was that Seaku wanted Farocan to hire and train Inuit fishermen, creating a pool of experienced offshore fishermen who consider the fishery their profession. Seaku in return would get a certain percentage of the sales from the shrimp product. After an agreement was reached, and the fishing vessel built, Inuit fishermen were recruited for some of the positions on the boat and fishing operations began. In the beginning, Koneak says they had no idea how Inuit would take to being out at sea for periods of up to six weeks at a time without touching land. "There was a lot of turnover at the start," says Marc Allard, General Manager of Seaku fisheries. "People thought it would be a great job. But once they got on the boat, and realized they couldn't get off it for a period of a month or so, it was a different story. Crew members must complete three fishing trips before being replaced and each trip lasts between three to five weeks depending on fishing." Koneak says those days are mostly gone. There is a lower turnover, and after ten years, a stable pool of fishermen has been established. "We are even getting a few officers now," says Koneak. The boat many Inuit fishermen have come to know is the "Aqviq." This 150 foot offshore vessel fishes the Makivik license managed by Seaku. It is a modern factory freezer trawler designed to harvest, process, freeze and package shrimp at sea (even in ice 3 feet thick) and cost in the neighbourhood of $15 million dollars to build. The vessel can accommodate as many as 25 people but usually fishes with a crew complement of 20-22 fishermen. The Aqviq sets out from ports in Atlantic Canada several times a year en route to the cold water shrimp fishing grounds in the Labrador Sea and in Davis Strait, between Baffin Island and Greenland. On average the Aqviq can hold up to 220 metric tons of product

per trip. Each license allows the Inuit owned companies to fish approximately 2,000 metric tons of shrimp annually. According to the Department of Fisheries and Oceans (DFO) these licenses can only land cold water shrimp, a product Marc Allard describes as sweeter tasting but smaller than warm water shrimp. The market for this product is predominantly Europe and Japan with new markets being developed in Asia. At present less than five per cent of the shrimp caught by Farocan is sold on the North American market.

On board the Aqviq, life is composed of basically three activities: working, eating, and sleeping. The vessel operates 24 hours a day and the fishermen work 12 hours a day on split shifts. They'll work six hours on, and six off, six on, six off. When there is a lot of product, they will work six on, six off, nine on, three off, and so on. Allard describes it as "hard physical work, the fishermen are on their feet all day, and if they are on deck it's also cold and wet. There's some danger involved as well. When the net comes up filled with several tons of shrimp they could be seriously or fatally injured if they get in the way of the steel cables used in hauling in the net, so the deckhands must be alert at all times."

Because it is a factory-freezer trawler, the Aqviq takes the shrimp from the sea and processes it on the spot. The shrimp are first sorted and separated into different size classes. The largest shrimp are destined for Japanese markets and are packed raw into one kilogram boxes and frozen. They are then packed into 12 kg master cartons. The large and medium shrimp are cooked in large vats of water and sent by conveyor belt through a blast freezer where they are individually quick frozen and immediately packed into 5 kg boxes. Once the shrimp are boxed and frozen, they are stored in the vessels large freezer rooms. The remaining small shrimp are frozen raw and packed in 30 kg bags where they will be sent to shrimp peeling plants. Finally, when the ship is full of product, they go into port and off load. For the crew, it is time to feel dry land again for a day or two before starting the next trip. After three trips have been completed, crew travel home for a much needed rest, while a new crew boards the vessel to begin another fishing expedition. Meanwhile, in the port itself, the shrimp are transferred to containers and shipped to their destination.

The Japanese buyers are very particular about their shrimp. They want the absolute best quality they can get. So. they often place their own technicians aboard the vessel to supervise this production. This product is usually sold before it leaves the boat and in this way there are no arguments about quality once it reaches Japan. A Danish company called F. Uhrenholt Fisk A/S handles the marketing and sales of all the product. Most of the shrimp is sold before it leaves the boat so that when it arrives in port, either Newfoundland, Nova Scotia or Greenland, the product is simply loaded into freezer containers and shipped to the markets. Marc Allard says when the vessels are fishing in the Davis Strait they usually land in Greenland. No matter where the vessel lands however the product is always landed as "Product of Canada" and as a result, we must pay

a 12% import tariff for all products entering the European Community.

When Seaku began fishing with Farocan ten years ago there were only four or five Inuit fishermen employed on the vessel but today it has as many as 12 Inuit. All first time fishermen must now successfully complete an "Orientation Program" designed to introduce the novice fishermen to life at sea but more importantly the many skills required for working on the vessel. Advanced training programs, co-ordinated by Unaaq, have helped promote the more serious fishermen and many now occupy better positions on the vessel, such as trawlermen–deckhands, fishing gear specialists, factory chiefs, and even a few officers. There are a few crew members of Faeroese origin working on the vessel who occupy only the most advanced positions, usually as Captain and Engineer. In the years ahead, Seaku plans to fill all positions on the vessel with Inuit crew members. We asked why the Faeroese are such great offshore fishermen. Jackie Koneak says, "They are the seamen of seamen. Their main business is offshore fishing and we have developed and maintained excellent working relations with them." Koneak says he has visited the small island country located in the North Atlantic Ocean between Scotland and Iceland. The Faroe Islands, like Greenland, is a self-governing territory in the kingdom of Denmark. Marc Allard explains the President of Farocan, Jogvan Kjolbro, had spent many years fishing in the same waters near Greenland, so he was very familiar with the area. The Faeroese have played an important role in developing the technology used aboard the offshore shrimp trawlers. "They have extensive experience and knowledge in harvesting and processing this product, and they know where the lucrative markets are as well," says Allard. There are 17 shrimp fishing licenses held by Canadian companies. All of the license holders have together formed an association called the Canadian Association of Prawn Producers (CAPP). The group meets on a regular basis to discuss quotas and other issues of concern to their industry. One of the most pressing concerns these days is the new $130,000 dollar annual license fee DFO plans to levy as of January 1, 1996. For Makivik, this fee will take a large chunk out of the $350,000 dollar annual royalty it receives from the shrimp fishing operation. These revenues are mostly used by Seaku to conduct community-based research and development projects and is considered an important source of revenue. Luckily, Seaku has recently obtained a permit to fish 1,000 metric tons of turbot. This will help the bottom line. A report prepared by John Angel, the Executive Director of CAPP, states that although CAPP does not object to the principle that the beneficiaries of the resource should pay a fair share of the costs of managing the fishery, we are very concerned about the approach taken by DFO on cost recovery initiatives and find their philosophy and process to be fundamentally flawed.

After ten years, Jackie Koneak calls the work done by Seaku a significant accomplishment. "We are employing over 100 people in Nunavik. That wasn't there before. At least two million dollars is being brought into Nunavik a year as a result." It takes capital to get the ball rolling. Makivik Corporation may have lost money fifteen years ago with Imaqpik, but with the initial investment in the licenses, and the human resources it has invested in, such as Marc Allard and Guy Préfontaine at Seaku, and Neil Greig at Unaaq, it has created ventures that have benefited Inuit, and has the potential to help other indigenous peoples around the globe. Seaku's model of holding a license, and finding the perfect match with a vessel owner has piqued the interest of other aboriginal groups abroad. The Mosquito Indians of Nicaragua are interested in learning how to develop their inshore fisheries based on a similar model. Marc Allard has visited this region twice to discuss potential projects with them, and Makivik Executives Jackie Koneak, Peter Adams, and Sheila Watt-Cloutier plan to make a return trip at the end of 1995, or early 1996 to continue this work. The international development work will be the topic of another installment on the tenth anniversary of Seaku Fisheries. We also intend to report on the research projects that have been undertaken by Seaku in Nunavik's coastal waters, and also on the work being done to train the Inuit fishermen, conducted by Unaaq, Seaku's 50% joint venture partner with Qiqiktaaluk Corporation.

(Makivik News, Winter 1995/1996, page 28)

Focusing upon Business Partnerships

A big step toward greater self sufficiency for Québec Aboriginals was taken when around 300 business minded individuals from all walks mingled for the Native Entrepreneurship and Partnerships Conference, held at the Radisson des Gouverneurs Hotel in Montréal, April 16-17. For these two days, invited experts spoke in their area of business interests to an audience of inquisitive listeners, which was followed by opportunities for questions from the floor. Then, participants would break into discussion groups in smaller meeting rooms and brainstorm about relevant obstacles and solutions. More intimate business contacts were made by those who met and exchanged business cards and ideas on a one-on-one basis in the hotel lobby and dining room between speaking and discussion sessions.

In his opening remarks to participants, Abel Kitchen, President of the First People's Business Association welcomed guests to what he called "the most important conference on Native entrepreneurship ever organized in Québec."

Although there had been past attempts to deal with Native economic development, this was the first gathering to actually focus on Native entrepreneurs and their present and potential business partners. Each individual participant was given access to other Native business people, to representatives of non-Native enterprises and to relevant federal and provincial government ministries. Guest speak-

ers shared their experience and expertise on the topics of natural resource exploitation (such as mining), tourism, agri-foods (such as wildlife harvesting), Aboriginal arts and crafts, and business financing. Government ministers at the conference were Canadian Indian Affairs (DIAND) Minister Ron Irwin; David Cliche, Québec Minister of Environment; and Rita Dionne-Marsolais, Québec Minister for Industry and Commerce.

Micheline L'Espérance-Labelle (President of Québécor DIL Multimedia, a company that produces educational software and computer applications) and Makivik Third Vice-President Mark T. Gordon, were the Honorary Co-Presidents of the conference.

Mark T. Gordon made a speech to inform individuals and companies who wish to do business in Nunavik of the concerns and priorities of Inuit in the region. Like other Aboriginal leaders at the conference, he asserted the pressing need to create employment for the young. Populations of Native youth and children are substantially larger than that of adults. In Nunavik, Inuit under 30 make up over 70%.

Most Inuit in Nunavik live below the poverty level in an area that has twice the cost of living and nearly twice the number of dependents relying on each wage earner, compared to the rest of Canada.

"Is it any wonder that we are concerned about economic development in Nunavik and that we are very interested to explore all possible avenues to create jobs and increase economic activity in our region?" he questions.

He pointed out the successes that Makivik has had with its subsidiary, Nunavik Arctic Foods, Inc (NAF). With the largest caribou population on earth, Nunavik has a high growth potential for bio food developments. Before any animal harvesting was carried out for NAF, however, "it was decided that proper wildlife management and the preservation of the species for future generations must always take precedence over monetary issues," he told the audience.

Mr. Gordon also outlined some other outstanding characteristics of an Inuit and non-Inuit joint venture. "There has to be mutual trust defined in the partnership agreement, and responsibilities need to be clearly defined between the two parties. Because the Inuit party is permanently tied to the region, they should have 51% ownership of the initiative and a clear buy-out clause in the agreement. Inuit should also take on greater responsibility of the operation as the technical knowledge is transferred through experience, and those who want to do business in Nunavik need to gain a sensitive understanding of the region, the people, and the culture in which they hope to operate," he says.

A very important aspect of the conference was the opportunity for participants to make direct contact with individuals from private companies or government departments who can influence the creation and growth of Native businesses.

Barbara Papigatuk, a KRG Employment and Training Counsellor from Salluit was there. She is responsible for employee recruitment for the Raglan project in Nunavik.

But as an employment counsellor, her interests extend to any potential job opportunities for residents of the region.

She says, "The networking aspect of the conference was most beneficial for me because I got to speak to people who are in positions of knowledge and have information about what employment developments to expect in the future."

"I was particularly interested to hear what they had to say about mining, due to the fact that there is a mine opening up in our back yard. But I was also there to hear about what other projects are happening in different parts of the country as well; what type of agreements have been made and what activities are taking place in the mining sector throughout Canada." She added, "It was a profitable experience."

Salluit Mayor Willie Keatainak, who has played a major role in negotiating with Falconbridge, was a key speaker on the mineral development panel. He reiterated the importance of maintaining good communications between outside entrepreneurs and Natives.

The Raglan Agreement was not Salluit's first encounter with such a project. An asbestos mine was exploited in the same general area for approximately 20 years from the early 1960s to about 1980, when relations between mining companies and Inuit were almost nonexistent, he told the audience.

At least in the Falconbridge example, this situation has made a turn around for the better. Daniel Gignac, Falconbridge Manager of Operations for the Raglan Project, was also on the mining panel. He says communication now begins well before deciding to go ahead with development, and partners on both sides need to be flexible and accommodating.

Other matters being addressed for the large scale mining project are environmental concerns and the need to identify project specific partnership opportunities (such as for catering, transportation, and road construction).

Willie Keatainak explained that Air Inuit, which has secured contract work at Raglan, is an exception to the norm because it is already a well established company. "In other fields of expertise, Inuit enterprises are few and those that do exist are probably under qualified and/or unable to carry out major works.

"To remedy the situation, joint ventures are being sought with different companies for work at Raglan. Our participation as partners in the development of the mine has yet to be developed, but the opportunities are there and we are willing and eager to undertake the necessary steps in order to benefit from the project," the Salluit mayor says.

As a final suggestion, Mr. Gignac of Falconbridge recommends to interested parties: "You should use the Raglan/Makivik Agreement as a model for developing your own sorts of partnership agreements with Native communities."

Attasi Pilurtuut was also in Montréal for the business conference. He works at the health services office in Kuujjuaq, and has a side interest in contracts for catering and construction.

As an observer at the conference, he was mainly curious about the bio-food industry and mining. As for the bio-foods, he wanted to see what measures are taken to prevent any risks to human health through proper handling of food products.

In regards to mining development in Nunavik, Attasi was there to find out what environmental studies are planned to ensure the least amount of environmental contamination. "When mining starts it creates pollution in the area. We Inuit who live in the region go out fishing and hunting in the mine area, so I am concerned more about that than the mining itself, because our livelihood will eventually be touched by the project," he says.

Also, he says, "I did attend one workshop where catering services were discussed. I was interested in trying to come up with a partnership program to get into a catering business at Falconbridge. Some (potential business partners) thought it would be too costly to operate, but in the long run I think that both parties would benefit from it because in the North, when restaurant and hotel businesses come around, it produces quite a bit of income."

Greater tourism developments could bring added clients for the hospitality industry in Nunavik. It was realized at the conference that transportation is one of the main drawbacks for tourism, that the industry is still quite fragile, but that there is a large potential market for tourists from the United States and Europe who are fascinated by Native cultures and their special knowledge of the environment.

Auriélien Gill, there as a guest speaker on tourism, is

involved in the aviation industry and is a professor of Native issues. He made the point that the Natives who welcomed and gave comfort to the first foreign visitors to this continent were actually the very pioneers in the tourism industry, and this tradition can be continued. "We (Canadian aboriginals) are asleep on a cultural treasure," he says.

One important objective of the conference was to break down barriers and stereotypes associated with the various cultures of people involved. "(We need to) once and for all destroy the myth that native money is easy money. Partnerships with Native partners are the same as any other partnerships. A key success factor is for the joint venture to use the strengths of the respective partners. They must each bring to the venture essential elements required for its success. Their respective strengths must complement and not overlap one another," said Mark T. Gordon.

Humour was applied extensively by many participants to loosen up what could easily have otherwise become a rather rigid meeting.

Crée leader Albert Diamond told of the farmer who had a problem with a certain beaver who kept rebuilding his dam and flooding the surrounding land. Every morning the farmer would break down the dam, only to find it rebuilt again the following day. He brought his complaint to a neighboring Crée, who advised the farmer to paint the beaver's head white. So the farmer caught the beaver, painted its head white, and released the animal. "Why didn't the beaver rebuild its dam again last night?" the grateful farmer asked his wise neighbor. "Simple," replied the Crée, "The beaver is a construction worker. Give him a white hat and he stops working."

DIAND Minister Ron Irwin was bestowed the status of Honourary Chief by the Frog Lake First Nation. The Minister shared that when he approached one Frog Lake respected pipe carrier to ask whether he would be given a special name in recognition of his new proud status, the elder replied: "We will call you Walking Eagle—because you are too fat to fly." (The Crées have actually given Irwin the name "Voice in the Rising Sun.") And, Mark T. Gordon, who once worked at one of the hunting camps near Ungava, told the story of one of his fellow Inuit guides. The guide and a strapping sports hunter were out on the land away from camp when the client from the south asked him if he knew the time of day. The Inuk looked up at the sky, then at his companion and replied, "Exactly 2:35 p.m." "How can you be so precise with the time by just looking at the sky?" "I looked at my wrist watch first," came the reply. We wish to thank those of you who have managed to remain interested in this article to the end, and if you have, you are probably looking at your own time piece with other things to do. If your interests lie in creating a business with a non-Native partner, know that there are others interested in the same goal. As the result of the Native Entrepreneurship and Partnerships Conference, discussions to find solutions for any concerns that you may have about such a venture have likely already begun.

(Makivik News, Summer 1996, page 29)

Pavement Project in Kuujjuaq

Development in Kuujjuaq, Nunavik's largest community, is progressing at rate that they are constantly showing even more resemblance to communities in southern
Canada. Municipal workers in the community expect that
the project of paving all the roads in the built up area there
(approximately 13 kilometers in all) should be completed
by the summer of 1997.

They estimate it will cost a total of $1,400,000 for the
project, not including the purchase of the asphalt plant
and paving equipment made previously, amounting to
$200,000. Most of the funding has come from a 1994-
1995 contract with the Department of National Defense
(DND) to clean up contaminated sites and remove barrels
and other scrap.

Ian Robertson, who works on municipal improvements
in Kuujjuaq, says the budgeted paving cost is approximately
$110 per meter, not including the preparation of the road
for asphalt which has been done, as much as possible, under
the road upgrading project funded by the Québec Municipal Affairs Department through KRG, at a total cost of
$4.2 million. About 3,200 barrels of asphalt were collected
under the DND project, 500 of which originated from
the last re-paving of the airport in 1987 and the contents
of these barrels could be used for asphalt as they were. Asphalt contained in the other barrels was older (from 1967
and before), and requires a polymer mixture to improve its

quality for paving.

During 1995, Kuujjuaq completed the paving of about 1.5 kilometers of roads at a cost of $440,000, including the start up and reconditioning of the plant, the purchase of 700 barrels of polymer asphalt (for mix) and other start up costs. Most time consuming to pave were the junctions at the intersections and the wider roads which receive the heaviest traffic. These areas will be completed first, so the project will speed up as workers get to work on the narrow streets.

This year, from June to October, about 10 local people were employed full time, with an opportunity to work on the roads at least 70 hours per week, weather permitting. Two other full-time jobs and four part-time jobs were created at a camp set up for the project, while a plant operator and a pave operator were hired from the south. Local personnel were also being trained to operate the plant and the paving equipment so Kuujjuaq will not need to hire these specialists from the south next year.

Less than halfway through the project, the dust level in Kuujjuaq has noticeably been reduced compared to previous years. This may also be partly due to the substantial efforts to grow grass and other vegetation on private plots.

Robertson says they expect that traffic regulations (The Highway Code) will be enforced more strongly by the Kativik Regional Police Force not only because of the pavement, but more because of the number of vehicles using the roads, which is always increasing. "We have not noticed any major change in peoples' driving habits since the new asphalt has been installed. The road to the airport has been paved since 1987, and some roads were paved last year, so people are used to driving on it. One big problem we have is with parents who allow very young kids (sometimes 5 or 6 years old) to drive (small) motorcycles as well as ride bicycles, unsupervised, on the roads," he maintains.

(Makivik News, Fall 1996, page 63)

Furniture Anyone???
By Bruno Pilozzi

For quite some time there has been discussion to increase the activity in the manufacturing sector of the Nunavik economy. The latest in these efforts is a household furniture, assembly and finishing operation in Salluit. This initiative has been the brainchild of Mark T. Gordon, Third Vice-President of Makivik, responsible for Economic Development.

There is a definite need for more variety of household furniture, obtainable by Nunavik residents at more affordable prices. In addition to the very limited furniture selection in the local Co-op and Northern stores are the very high prices for these items. Because of the limited market in Nunavik, transportation makes up a large part of the retail price.

The concept for the pilot operation in furniture assembly was to create local jobs and reduce the cost of transporting furniture. The materials imported to Nunavik would be unfinished basic components, shipped in compact boxes, utilizing a fraction of the packaging required for a finished unit. For the initial pilot operation a sample selection of furniture was chosen to demonstrate the quality, pricing structure, and ease of assembly. The selection included a queen size bed, a dresser, a coffee table, a 10 person dining table, a six person kitchen table and two styles of chairs that come in sets of six.

Kululak Ilisituk, a Kuujjuaq resident who originally came from Salluit, was chosen to be trained in a brief furniture finishing course in Montréal. Kululak then went to Salluit and was responsible for the actual assembly and finishing of the sample units. The reactions from everyone who examined the samples were extremely positive.

The Qarqalik Landholding Corporation of Salluit will own and operate this new business venture. The Kativik Regional Development Council has provided, and shall continue to provide, the Qarqalik workers with management and bookkeeping assistance. Full commercial operations are expected to begin in September, 1998. Already discussions have begun regarding the possibility of supplying furniture to the communities south of Salluit where the units could be transported there on Air Inuit's backhaul flights at reduced cargo rates.

(Makivik News, Fall 1997, page 49)

Sakkuk Landholding

Two main subsidiaries of the Sakkuq Landholding Corporation of Kuujjuaraapik are up and running, creating a few jobs and some local economic stimulation. These two companies are the Qilalugak Hotel and Resto-Pub in Kuujjuaraapik and an outfitting enterprise called Nunami Inc. based at Lake Mollet, south of the community. In terms of the success of Landholding Corporations in Nunavik, Sakkuq is doing well for their beneficiaries.

With advice and support from the Makivik Legal Department, beginning about four years ago, Sakkuq began to improve its organization. Makivik has also provided some venture capital for these businesses.

As an independent accounting consultant, Michel Lemieux keeps the books for Sakkuq. Lemieux estimates that both subsidiary companies should receive a combined revenue of around $1 million for this year.

Alec Tuckatuck is the President of the Sakkuq Landholding Corporation of Kuujjuaraapik. He wants Sakkuq beneficiaries to realize that their goal is to have the Landholding Corporation's subsidiary companies managed completely by Inuit someday. He says right now there are no Inuit available in Kuujjuaraapik with the necessary expertise to manage these positions at the Resto-Pub or at Nunami. "It will be done in the future but those things take time for us to learn about," he says. So they hire from elsewhere, and hope that one day more Inuit will become educated and eager to be employed in these top positions.

Qilalugak Resto-Pub and Hotel

The Qilalugak Resto-Pub and Hotel, formerly the Sin-ittavik Hotel, was purchased by Sakkuq in 1996 and re-opened under new management in 1997.

Jeannine Petit, who has lived in Kuujjuaraapik for the past seven years, is the manager for Qilalugak. Many who have taken adult education courses in Kuujjuaraapik recognize her as the cook from the student residence.

Qilalugak Resto-Pub bar is open each evening until 10:30 pm except Sundays. The dining room opens for lunch and again for supper. They do not serve breakfast, as Petit explains, there is normally only enough people in the community eating out for breakfast to support one restaurant, and they go to Kuujjuaraapik's Coffee Shop up the street. The two or three choice buffet and exclusive menu at the dining room provides a balance to the fast food menu served at the Coffee Shop. This arrangement works fine in Kuujjuaraapik which has just two restaurants. Eleven people work at the Resto-Pub most times, and 16 in the summer.

With a maximum of 120 seats, the Resto-Pub also serves the community by catering to special group celebrations. One Sunday last spring the staff showed up to prepare a banquet for hockey teams participating in the Nunavik Cup there. Qilalugak orders their food from Val d'or.

"The people here are proud to have a nice restaurant

with good food," Jeannine says, "They find that coming here is like going to a restaurant down south."

"Touch wood," Petit says, tapping her knuckles on the edge of a sturdy bar table, "We have not had a fight in here yet." Drinking and rowdiness seem to go together. Alec Tuckatuck theorizes that operating liquor establishments in Kuujjuaraapik reduces the illegal importing of liquor and other mind altering substances from the south. "We are not promoting alcohol. We are just saying it's ready for you if you want it, and use it the right way," he says. Since the 1950s, Kuuiiuaraapik has a social club besides the Resto-Pub, which also serves liquor. It has been open to public members since 1975. The Oilalugak dining room and bar are decorated in a trendy manner. Inside, it is distinguishable from other sporty bars in the south by the Inuit and Crée paraphernalia, costumes and taxidermy displayed. The establishment is housed in a building that was once a fire hall owned by the American Air force, then the Canadian Air force. An official grand opening for the Qilalugak Resto-Pub is planned for July 2. 1998. The hotel is comprised of two Air Force surplus buildings know as E-wing and D-wing. E-wing is beautiful inside because it was newly renovated. D-wing needs fixing up, but is kept clean and maintained well enough to sleep guests when the nicer building is full. There are plans to expand and renovate once it becomes more affordable for Sakkuq.

Alec Tuckatuck says when the hotel operation was conceived there was a lot of talk in town about a major Hydro-Québec project at Great Whale and Sakkuq expected there to be a lot of people coming in for that. The Landholding Corporation had its eyes set on accommodating Hydro professionals. Formerly, the hotel was intended to be a joint venture with the previous owners. However, as plans evolved, Sakkuq became the sole proprietor. It was also decided to start up a Resto-Pub.

Annie Ittoshat has been working as a server at the Qilalugak restaurant for the past year, a job she prefers over tending to customers at the bar. She says serving those who come to eat in the restaurant provides her the chance to meet new people, which she enjoys. Her split shift working day gives her more time to spend with family.

Annie used to work as a housing clerk for the municipality and, before that, she began a degree at college in Montréal. It's hard to get back into school once a person has rooted themselves into the work world, she finds, but for now she is comfortable at Qilalugak. She says one of the most difficult aspects of working is having to say goodbye to colleagues who move on to other occupations.

Sakkuq of Kuujjuaraapik also has plans to develop a goose hunting operation from their hotel in the community. It would mean that Qilalugak would apply to become licensed as an outfitter. They would bring goose hunters, who arrive in Kuuuuaraapik from Montréal by regular commercial flights, out to the Hudson's Bay coast by boat in the fall. This operation should also create spin-off opportunities for the economy of Kuujjuaraapik, such as in the sale of arts and crafts and other retail outlets.

Getting Started at Nunami

Sakkuq first looked at Mollet Lake as a potential outfitting site about three years ago, when the Makivik Corporation still maintained a tourism department. Peter Palmer, who was with Makivik Tourism then, is now an independent consultant overseeing the development of the Sakkuq subsidiary project through his company, Palmer and Associates. Palmer received this contract from the Sakkuq Landholding of Kuuuuaraapik on August 16, 1997.

What has turned into a 100% Inuit owned, eye opening venture for many associated with the outfitting business, Nunami got its start when Sakkuq sent a party of outfitting specialists to do a primary survey of the Hydro-Québec site at Mollet Lake three years ago. The site had been abandoned for over four years and was deteriorated by nature and vandals.

Did it have potential as a tourism site for the Hudson's Bay communities? Umiujaq and Inukjuak were also interested at first. The Nunami Camp is now completely owned by the Sakkuq Landholding Corporation of Kuujjuaraapik.

"We went in there and inventoried every nail, plumbing fixture and piece of furniture and estimated what it would require to bring the infrastructure up to par," says Peter Palmer, who Makivik had lent to Sakkuq for the survey back then. During that first visit the group also started to clean up some of the mess around there.

They concluded that the project had definite potential, so they went back the following year to make a further assessment. The whole season was spent cleaning up and.

at the same time, a lot of wood and other equipment was shipped in to begin renovations and to solidify the infrastructure.

A complete study was done in the area on the fishing potential, Palmer says. They cross referenced government reports on migration characteristics of caribou in the area, and other natural geographic attractions.

Some of the original infrastructure was recycled, and other buildings were renovated. The Mollet Lake site, which originally cost Hydro-Québec around $1 million to construct, was used as a base camp to study water characteristics for the power corporation. "A lot of the Hydro people are very happy that the camp is taking on a new life." Palmer says, "Basically, we took this abandoned infrastructure which had the doors banging in the wind and the spirit gone from it, and we have started to turn it into something of pride for the community."

The Facility

Nobody is more proud of Nunami's progress than Alec Tuckatuck. "We nave been working on an outfitting business which is also a job creation program for the beneficiaries, and now we have a first class facility," Tuckatuck describes. "Nunami provides everything a guest needs in order to hunt and live good. After a nice long hard day, you have showers, good food, and good lodging in that camp. We also have guides who really know the territory." Tuckatuck says there is a growing demand for tourists who want to visit out of the way places such as in Nunavik.

Nunami's Mollet Lake Lodge is the closest outfitting infrastructure to a road that is connected to the south in Nunavik, 127 miles north of the LG-4 road, and 142 miles north east of the road from LG-2.

Situated in proximity to a road and to the airport at Radisson has made it more affordable to bring in equipment and building materials. Loads can be trucked up and then air lifted or hauled to the camp by snowmobile.

Located just below the tree line, the territory is more wooded than most of sub-Arctic Nunavik, good for shelter and campfires. There are also a lot of sand beaches, with many rolling hills but less tracts of rock than further north. The warmer climate also gives Nunami a longer period of time to operate with open waters.

In a vast unspoiled environment with so much moving water in its system, Nunami is at one of the best natural brook trout networks in North America. Other native fish species there include lake trout and northern pike.

Mollet Lake Lodge is presently equipped to bunk 40 clients at a time. "We are looking at other kinds of tourists besides hunting or fishing; things like adventure tourism, sight seeing or bird watching," Alec Tuckatuck says. "It's time to open up the tourism industry here wisely and fairly."

Plans and Potential

Mollet Lake Lodge officially opened for sports fishing on July 15th, with plans to remain in full operation until October 6th. From the beginning of last year, when they first started marketing, until mid–May, Nunami registered 150 clients. Three quarters of them are strictly interested in fishing and the balance, hunting. The caribou hunt starts in the fall.

Ninety percent of their guests come from the United States. During their primary marketing efforts, Mollet representatives canvassed at many trade shows throughout the north eastern United States and Texas. Most of their clientele were recruited at these shows and through other agents which were contacted by Peter Palmer, who manages promotion for Nunami.

Mollet has also attracted the attention of Mirage Outfitters. Located on the LG-4 road, 125 miles south of Mollet Lake. Mirage deals strictly in winter caribou hunting for tourists and is one of the largest outfitters in the province. Last year they received around 2,700 hunters.

The company is interested in utilizing Mollet as a destination to begin guiding their hunters from the LG-4 road by snowmobile. "What this means," Palmer concludes, "Is that Mollet Lake Lodge is in the process of becoming a northern motel specializing in winter caribou hunting."

Nunami promoters are also working with the Crée and Inuit to provide an experience with these local Indigenous cultures for European visitors. "This area is the only place in Nunavik where you have a meshing of these two cultures," Palmer says.

One important success at Mollet was last winter when they hosted the Nunavik Arctic Foods (1998) Ltd. caribou harvest. It was the first major contract for Nunami.

Nunami's main goal for this year is to create six Inuit jobs for a six to eight month period at Mollet, and a career possibility for one youth in Kuujjuaraapik.

Palmer says, "If you can operate a camp at 45 degrees below zero, as we have proven to do, with flush toilets, hot running showers and everything else you would find in a motel, then it is easy money to do it in the summer and fall."

He summarizes, the goal of Nunami is to operate Mollet as a four season, all purpose infrastructure that is diversified into commercial production of meats for the region, general hunting and fishing, and "last but not least" the pure adventure tourism in the area. "And," he adds, "We are right on track!"

Makivik has provided technical support to the Sakkuq Landholding Corporation as well as support in the form of loans and loan guarantees in the vicinity of $1 million for the realization of both the Nunami Outfitting camp and the Qilalugak Hotel and Resto-Pub projects.

(Makivik News, Summer 1998, page 5)

Investor's Interest

Le Fonds régional de solidarité Nord-du-Québec made a presentation, entitled "Powering Job Creation," to the Makivik Executive in Kuujjuaq on October 6th. Their purpose was to explain what the Fonds régional is for and to hear how the residents of Nunavik think their "financial instruments" could be modified to suit the region. It was their fourth visit to Nunavik since January, 1998.

Their key objectives are to create jobs and training opportunities, and to coach business entrepreneurs. They are interested in economic development and in acting as a complimentary fund to development organizations already in place in Nunavik.

The Fonds régional invests money through unsecured loans or shares, and provides management help for enterprises in which they invest.

The money for investments comes from the Fonds de solidarité des travailleurs du Québec (F.T.Q.). The $6 million available for investments in Nunavik is private money from small investors, and not from subsidies or from the provincial or federal governments.

Claude Ladoucer, Fonds Régional General Manager, says they are interested in Nunavik because it has a significant need for jobs for young people and because there are interesting opportunities for economic development in (certain) sectors.

A confident sounding Mr. Ladoucer stated: "I will really

try to find a way the Fond Régional can help Nunavik. I know it is difficult. My job is not to look at the problem—it is to find a solution."

But there are problems to attend to. The Makivik Executive members pointed out several conditions that make running an industry in Nunavik more difficult than in other Aboriginal communities further south. There is a lack of banking services, multiple layers of taxes, extremely far distances to travel and to ship things, and no buildings available for rent which means an entrepreneur has to construct their own. "You have to become both a landlord and a business owner, so there are very high costs even to start a small business," said Makivik Third Vice President Mark T. Gordon.

The Fond Régional realized the necessity, as well as the obstacles, for keeping in touch with Nunavik residents. They plan to make more frequent field trips in the region, as well as to have their information distributed in Inuktitut. They also intend to foster more frequent exchanges with Nunavik institutions such as the Nunavik Investment Corporation and Makivik Corporation.

Nunavik residents may call KRDC for more information about the Fond Régional.

(Makivik Magazine, Winter 1998-1999, page 43)

Celebrating Inukjuak's New Recreation Centre

On December 18, 1998 the Makivik executives, the chairman of Kativik Regional Government, and various employees of both organizations chartered one of Air Inuit's Twin Otters to join the people of Inukjuak to celebrate the opening of their new recreational building.

The building sits on top of a hill. Its big and beautiful, splashed with fun and cheerful colors. The gymnasium has high ceilings and bleachers where people can watch activities below. A large reception area at the entrance has large windows that allow natural light in, with a spectacular view of the community and the river.

At around 7:00 Mayor Siasi Smiler made a speech at the entrance before everybody did a tour of the facility. Following the speech there was a display of fireworks. Then the doors were officially opened for everyone to see the Inukjuak Community Centre.

A variety of talented Inukjuak artists performed live music. There were square dances while Andrew Atagotaalok played the accordion. There was a draw for a pair of Air Inuit tickets. Tea and different kinds of bannock and cookies were offered.

The building was designed by an architectural company whose buildings are all over the North. Fournier Gersovitz Moss Architects have also designed the Kuujjuaq Forum, the daycare centres in Inukjuak and Kuujjuaq, the terminal building in Iqaluit, and numerous others.

Most people spoke about how the Inukjuak Community Centre will have a positive impact on the young people and how it will allow them to have something to do and somewhere to go. Inukjuak Mayoress Siasi Smiler stated, "Its beautiful, I am ecstatic, it allows freedom to young people and its proudly appreciated."

Pita Aatami and Johnny Adams both gave a speech before departing back to Kuujjuaq. Johnny was proud for the people of Inukjuak. Pita stated that the building does not come from Makivik, but from the people themselves.

Nonetheless, Makivik contributed $2 million. There will be an attempt to obtain the money for the building from the provincial government. According to the James Bay and Northern Québec Agreement, the provincial government must provide recreational centres for Nunavik's population. Despite the agreement, Makivik has paid for all of Nunavik's arenas and various recreation centres totaling $25.8 million.

(Makivik Magazine, Spring 1999, page 33)

Makivik's New Joint-Venture Companies With the Inuit of Nunavut
By Stephen Hendrie

The day before Nunavut officially became a territory, Makivik signed two joint-venture agreements with Inuit birthright companies in Nunavut. They both involve the sea in some way. They are Nunavut Eastern Arctic Shipping (NEAS), and Natsiq Investment Corporation.

Nunavut Eastern Arctic Shipping

This joint shipping venture between Inuit birthright corporations and a southern partner has been operating since 1997. Makivik entered into the partnership in March 1999 by becoming one-third shareholders of Nunavut Umiaq Corporation, which in turn owns 60% of NEAS. The original owners of Nunavut Umiaq Corporation are Qikiqtaaluk Corporation (Inuit of Baffin Island), and Sakku Corporation (Inuit of Kitikmeot). Montréal-based Transport Nanuk owns the remaining 40% of NEAS. Transport Nanuk is owned 50% by Logistec Corporation of Montréal, and 50% by Northwest Company, based in Winnipeg.

Makivik became a partner in the joint venture to extend business opportunities beyond the Nunavut settlement area to include Nunavik. Pita Aatami says, "Shipping is a big part of northern life. It is logical to get into the shipping business as there are no roads linking our region

to the south." It was also a natural investment for Makivik Corporation as Transport Nanuk is based in Montréal, and has been involved in northern shipping for over 40 years prior to the joint venture with Inuit.

The main activity of business is the shipping of cargo from Montréal to the Eastern Arctic. Two ice-class vessels are in operation. The M.V. Lucien Paquin is 450 feet long, and has the capacity to carry 16,000 to 18,000 cubic metres of cargo. It is the largest general cargo ship servicing the Arctic, and has an Ice Class 1 classification. It was built in Sweden in 1969. The ship is well known in Nunavik communities. The M.V. Aivik is a newer ship, built in 1980 in France to transport the Arian Space Shuttle. It has a capacity of 10,000 to 12,000 cubic metres of cargo, and roll-on-roll-off capability. A rear-hinged door easily permits the shipment of heavy equipment such as a 60 ton rock crusher. Its two cranes can be combined to lift 310 tons.

From June to late September, both ships will be busily loading cargo in Montréal, and then sailing around the Gulf of St. Lawrence, up along the coast of Labrador, and then onwards to destinations in Nunavik and Nunavut. The first scheduled stop is in Iqaluit on July 2nd for the M.V. Aivik, following a closing date of June 25th at the port of Montréal.

With years of experience, NEAS is able to provide full service for northern shipping. There are few docking facilities in the North—Nunavik or Nunavut. Loading the ship in Montréal has to be done with the knowledge that unloading in each community is done with barges. As well, cargo to the North includes a wide variety of goods, from vehicles to houses. Not all of it is placed inside containers.

A priority for NEAS is to establish a program to train Inuit for technical certificates and diplomas in Nautical Science and Technology. NEAS is working with the Marine Institute of Memorial University in Newfoundland to provide the courses. The first step will be to recruit candidates for the various disciplines, which include Nautical Science, Marine Engineering, and Electro-Mechanical Engineering. The next step will be to decide the optimum method to deliver the courses—either to send candidates to Newfoundland, or to bring instructors to the North and provide the courses at Arctic College in Iqaluit.

Natsiq Investment Corporation

This joint venture aims to revive markets for seal products. The days of the Hudson's Bay Company buying stretched and skinned seal pelts are long gone. In its heyday, over 26,000 seal pelts were sold per year in Nunavik. The average price per skin was about $40. That was back in 1968. Now, the price per skin has dropped to below $10. Markets have been decimated by anti-sealing, and animal rights groups.

Natsiq is owned equally by Makivik Corporation, Sakku Investments Corporation, and Qikiqtaaluk Corporation. There are six members of the Board of Directors. For Makivik they are Pita Aatami, and George Berthe. The Sakku representatives are Joe Kaludjak, and Steve Mapsalak. At Qikiqtaaluk Corporation the representatives are

Jerry Ell and Johnny Mike.

The project is ambitious. The proposal is to harvest about 2,000 seals per month to process meat, oil, bone, organs, and pelts. Currently, the business activity consists of identifying and developing markets for the seal products in China, and in North America if changes are made to the Marine Mammal Protection Act.

Natsiq aims to develop a processing facility in the Arctic in order to retain the processing jobs within the Natsiq group of development corporations. At present, a plant on the island of Newfoundland is being explored as a possible start-up site to process the seals, and to develop training and job opportunities.

The proposal is to harvest about 2,000 seals per month to process meat, oil, bone, organs, and pelts.

The seal population has grown since the decline of the fur market, and major protests by animal rights groups. In the Atlantic and Arctic Canada, the total seal population is estimated to be 8 million seals. Ringed seals, found in the Arctic, are the most abundant species of seal in the northern hemisphere. Ringed seals are the most important species for the Inuit economy, for their meat, skin, and blubber.

A seal is composed of 39% meat, 29% fat and oil, 4% bones, 20% organs, and 8% pelt. In terms of usage, 98% of a seal can be processed into consumable products. The meat can be used for human and animal consumption. The fat and oil can also be used for human consumption, and industrial use. All of the pelt and bone can be processed, and 98% of the organs can be processed.

The business plan is based on paying hunters for the whole seal rather than just the pelt. Natsiq estimates that by processing the meat, fat and oil, bones, organs, guts, and pelt, the company will be profitable taking into consideration transportation of the seal from the field to the processing plant, processing costs, marketing, and distribution. Calculations have been made based on average weights of seals, from 100 to 140 lbs.

The long-term goal is to process as much of the seal as possible. The short-term focus is on the development of seal-oil capsules, which contain Omega-3, a pharmaceutical ingredient that reduces the risk of heart disease. The target market is Asia, notably in China, Hong Kong, Singapore, and Taiwan. Preventive medicines, such as seal-oil capsules, are popular in Asia. The US market is not open to the product because the Marine Mammal Protection Act prevents the sale of seal products in the US.

In 1999, about 500 seals will be harvested for seal-oil capsules. The first samples have been processed in Newfoundland. The goal for the year 2000 is to process 5,000 seals. Assuming markets develop as planned, a primary processing plant could be operational in the Arctic by the summer of 2001.

The emphasis in both of these joint ventures is to gain control of a sector of the economy that is vital to the Inuit at this time. Shipping to the Arctic has occurred for decades. NEAS brings Inuit ownership of the activity.

Sealing is basic to the Inuit lifestyle. Developing a new market for the product in the modern context is a challenge Natsiq Investment Corporation aims to accomplish in the years to come.

(Makivik Magazine, Summer 1999, page 36)

Sammy Kudluk

Doing Business With the Inuit: Gaining Access to the North

By Lucy Grey

A symposium called "Doing Business with Inuit: Gaining Access to the North" was held on May 27, 1999 in Calgary, Alberta. The Calgary Chamber of Commerce hosted the symposium. Inuit Taparisat of Canada and the Royal Bank organized the event. All four Inuit regional organizations across Canada and southern businesses were participants.

The reason for the symposium is that Corporate Canada is realizing that the aboriginal communities in Canada are full of business opportunities. A symposium similar to this one was held with the Métis and First Nations. The attention on the creation of Nunavut has heightened the interest shown by southern businesses.

Corporate Canada is realizing that Inuit are in control of natural resources found in their homelands and a cooperative relationship with Inuit is necessary to do business. As Okalik Eegeesiak, President of ITC stated, "Development is not happening to us, it's happening with us." The symposium is an attempt to help Inuit and Corporate Canada interact with one another in hopes of establishing business partnerships.

The symposium reflects the ending of an era of where Inuit had no control or say on what occurred in their homeland. Up until the signing of the James Bay and

Northern Québec Agreement, Inuit across Canada have had no active participation in key decisions that would affect their social, cultural, economic, and spiritual lives. The land claim agreements that followed have helped ensure that Inuit are guaranteed employment and training, compensation money, co-managing with governments on environmental and social issues, control over large scale resource development, and preferences to grant Inuit contracts. This would make it inevitable for southern businesses to go into partnership with Inuit to be able to take advantage of opportunities in the North.

Despite specific tools designed to build and promote the Inuit economy, many challenges are still faced. The wage economy is still dominated by the public services sector, there is a high rate of unemployment, a very young population that is growing rapidly, high cost of living and transportation, isolation, poor communication linkages, shortage of housing and daycare, a low rate of educated Inuit, and difficulty accessing banking and financing services.

In order for the aboriginals to overcome economic development obstacles, the Royal Commission on Aboriginal People has recommended that the Department of Indian Affairs and Northern Development let go of the control they exercise. The right to self-govern should be granted and provide block funds to aboriginal programs that support economic development. It is also recommended that the estimated $80 million traditional wildlife harvesters economy within Inuit communities be supported.

Many speeches were presented during the symposium

and exchange of information occurred among the participants. The key speakers were: Pita Aatami, President, Makivik Corporation; Charles Coffey, Executive Vice President, Royal Bank; Okalik Eegeesiak, President, Inuit Taparisat Canada; John McCallum, Chief Economist, Royal Bank; William Barbour, President, Labrador Inuit Association; Nellie Cournoyea, Chair/CEO, Inuvialuit Regional Corporation; Jerry Ell, President, Qikitaaluk Corporation; Sheila Watt-Cloutier, Vice-President for Canada of the Inuit Circumpolar Conference; Charlie Lyall, President, Kitikmeot Corporation; Nancy Karetak-Lindell, Member of Parliament for Nunavut; and Chesley Anderson, Advisor and chief negotiator for the Labrador Inuit Association.

The symposium was an excellent opportunity for Pan Arctic Inuit Logistics to launch their website that lists all the Inuit businesses across Canada. In addition, PAIL and ITC held their Board of Directors meetings to save on costs.

In conclusion, Inuit have been given specific tools to take control over developments that occur in their homelands. Taking control over economic development being the essential part by deciding on how to spend it. This also means the right to self-government. The goals could be reached through greater freedom and education.

(Makivik Magazine, Summer 1999, page 46)

Economic Development Projects

Last spring a clothing project survey form was distributed to all the readers of the *Makivik Magazine* in order to see how much interest there is in Nunavik to start up a cottage clothing business by Inuit sewers in the region. Considering the weak response to this effort, Victoria Okpik, who is employed by the corporation to work on this special project, spurred other residents to take part in the survey over the telephone. The results of this survey illustrates that Nunavik women have considerable experience in sewing. Makivik is grateful to all those who participated.

Of the people surveyed, 25% of the respondents were "very interested" in working at a sewing project and 48% of respondents were "somewhat interested." This total response of 73% has encouraged Makivik's economic development department to pursue the project with greater seriousness. Early last November, they made a presentation to the board of directors at the budget meeting in Montréal. The presentation, complete with a simple analysis report, a sewing machine, and two professionally created parkas from Victoria Okpik were reviewed by the Makivik board of directors. Seymour Gladman (a volunteer consultant from CESO Aboriginal Services), and Victoria Okpik and Charles Dorais from the economic development department made the presentation.

The feasibility study recommends a cottage type industry whereby women could make parkas at home—an enterprise which would fit in well with the typical northern lifestyle. It was realized that there could be a central location for the project to handle matters such as sales, designing, distribution, shipping, receiving, storage, training and quality control. The project could forseeably provide four full-time positions as well as 30 part-time sewing jobs initially.

It was found that parkas would be the best product to begin with, with each one marketed as a unique work of art as well as a functional garment to be worn in the cold. Possibly a photograph and short biography of the person who made the coat could be affixed for the customer to appreciate. Designs were also presented for a "Nunavik" brand label for the garments.

To start, these parkas would be sold to people within Nunavik, branching out to tourists visiting the region, and then possibly to the outside using an internet site to advertise the product. Beyond that, the Nunavik made garments could even be marketed through specialty boutiques in the south. It was recommended that parkas would be the best to start with, then mitts, and other sewn articles as well. Preliminary research has shown that there are a number of retailers in the south who are interested in purchasing unique Inuit parkas and amoutiks in various sizes on a continuous basis, which are presently unobtainable. Given the low investment required and the potential benefits, Makivik's economic development department is strongly in favour of going ahead with the clothing project. The next step will be to prepare a detailed business plan and look into possible funding sources for start-up costs. The study will also include market research and an analysis of competing northern clothing producers.

Makivik's economic development department has gone ahead and built three sewing/woodworking workshops in Salluit, Inukjuak and Kangirsuk. The new industrial workshops, which were expected to be completed by mid-December, are 70 feet by 30 feet, and of very high quality fabrication and design. Local workers were employed as much as possible for their construction. The three buildings are laid out with two identical sections and a service area in the middle. They are primarily intended for use by sewers on one side and by woodworkers on the other.

With plans for a regional clothing production underway, the workshops might also be used as centres for the project. However, one other option may be to rent one side of the workshops to small businesses. The leases would be for a limited time, giving a chance for other businesses to lease the premises during their start-up years. In this way, it is expected that the project will foster economic development by providing small businesses with a place to operate. Makivik Corporation will pay building operating costs during the first year. The estimated cost for each workshop is $350,000. Furthermore, the Makivik board of directors accepted a budget from the economic development department to furnish the workshops with equipment. Discussions have also taken place about the eventual transfer of the workshops to the communities.

(Makivik Magazine, Winter 1999-2000, page 12)

Inukshuk Productions Inc.

Andre Brassard's determination to make a vision come true— "Worldwide awareness of Inuit culture through Inuit music"— along with support and direction from various Nunavik artists, has given birth to Inukshuk Productions Inc. Their recording and production studio rivals most found in urban centres. André lives in Inukjuak with his wife, Mary Naktiailuk, and their two children.

Their studios boast a long list of specialized recording and production equipment. They have a computerized 40 channel recording mixer with digital and analog mastering equipment; a nonlinear computer editing system and Sony digital video camera; a Roland XP-80 synthesizer which has over 1200 sound effects; a Remo/Sabian set of drums, a Yamaha base guitar and a Fender solo guitar. They also have a soundproof recording room and an interview recording room for making video clips and television programs.

The day when Inukshuk Productions can start burning their own CDs in Inukjuak is foreseeable. They say it is also foreseeable that both their distribution volume and the caliber of their recorded artists will attain such a viable level as to permit Inukshuk to employ a few dozen highly skilled technologists in the region. Inukshuk Productions is capable and eager to further develop their training curriculum and facilities, thus making it possible for all Inuit students wishing to enter or further a career in music recording and production to do so.

Within five years, Inukshuk Productions Inc. has recorded numerous new talents and is exporting worldwide. Their albums have been exported as far away as Saudi Arabia, Europe, Asia, and locations in North and South America.

They are producing music video clips of Inuit artists and a television series of seven biographical interviews of the same Inuit artists, as they stand in today's Canadian music industry. These videos are produced in Inuktitut with English subtitles or translations.

For marketing reasons, they hope to eventually have translations in other languages spoken in countries buying these recordings. While intended to be seen primarily on TV stations and other broadcasting organizations worldwide, their video clips will also be made available to anybody. These items will be distributed throughout Nunavik and Nunavut by the Northern Stores and the Co-op Stores.

Inukshuk Productions Inc. relies on serious granting organizations to survive and develop. Such government funding is used to help in improving equipment, facilities and staff quarters. Along the way, they have received support from organizations such as Air Inuit and First Air, KRG, KRDC, KSB, The Department of Indian and Northern Affairs, Aboriginal Business Canada and the Canada Council. Other music oriented organizations such as SODEC, MusicAction, and Videofact have also been very supportive.

Their existing distribution network and partnerships include Inukshuk Distribution (Northern Canada and

Greenland, Alaska and USA), Hardel Muzik (southern Canada), Zango Music (USA), and Tandem Music (World-wide).

Inukshuk productions Inc. has 15 registered sub-divisions, preserving the name "Inukshuk" within the music industry. Eight of these divisions are presently active: Inukshuk Distribution, Inukshuk Publishing, Inukshuk Records, Inukshuk Studio, Inukshuk Management, Inukshuk Music Equipment, Inukshuk Video Production, and Inukshuk Television Production.

Inukshuk Productions Inc. provides work for eight employees. They were the recipients of the Mishtapew 1997 Exportation Award from the First Peoples Business Association.

Inukshuk's year 2000 discovery is Henoch Townley, a young Inuk from Labrador. His composing talent is only surpassed by his determination to succeed, which he has proven in very concrete ways.

André Brassard says they provide two general service arrangements for Inuit artists wanting to record. First, artists may rent their studio for $85 per hour where they can produce a master copy of their recording from which they may get reproductions done. If they are renting a studio, they should be sure they are ready to play. "Rehearse using a metronome," André advises, "The better prepared, the cheaper the studio time."

The second option is that an artist can sign on with Inukshuk Productions Inc. as a label, which is somewhat more complicated. André says before signing on, the artist must first acquire and study a copy of the book, Successful Artist Management, which he describes as "the Bible of the music Industry."

Inukshuk is also producing an Inuktitut show about the music industry to be aired on the Aboriginal Peoples Television Network. It is intended as an educational program on the music industry for the Inuit.

"There are a lot of artists in Nunavik, if they could realize the potential. For an artist who is serious and who has the right attitude and wants to play their music, it is unlimited what can be done," says André. "We are growing and expanding. Getting better and better equipment."

(Makivik Magazine, Spring/Summer 2000, page 42)

Brand New Gymnasiums for Kangirsuk and Puvirnituq

Upon the invitation from the municipalities of Kangirsuk and Puvirnituq, Makivik President Pita Aatami, along with Vice-President and Head of Economic Development Mark T. Gordon, and Chattel's Director of Projects René Ouellette, attended the opening of new gymnasiums for both communities.

Held on November 20, the opening in Kangirsuk was inaugurated with the traditional ribbon cutting, accomplished by an elder and a youth. Speeches were also done by Kangirsuk Mayor Joseph Annahatak, Makivik Board member Martha Kauki, a couple of community members and Makivik President Pita Aatami. Inside the gymnasium, lots of mattaq was served to the community for the special event, along with cooked meals. The elders had a special spot to enjoy the yummiest part of a beluga. The feast was topped off with a table size cake. In appreciation for the new gym, the municipality treated their guests with hand made gifts. René Ouellette received a nassaq printed with the name Chartel. Victor Mesher, who was the liason between the municipality of Kangirsuk, Makivik and Chartel, was surprised with a homemade parka, while Pita Aatami proudly received a kakivak and savik. The gymnasium, now called the Community Hall, was named after the recreation centre that was demolished in 1986.

Puvirnituq had also requested a gymnasium for their

population. Before, the only source of recreation facility Puvirnituq had available was the school gymnasium. The well respected elder Aisa Qoperqualuk did the ribbon cutting with a heartfelt speech, telling the crowd how today's generation should be grateful for so much comfort. He also shared his personal experience living in an igloo, his appreciation to the qulliq that provided him with light and heat. He brought the crowd to the past and then back to the present, appreciating what is now provided. Puvirnituq Mayor Aisara Kenuayuak and Pita Aatami also did the honors. After the ribbon cutting, everybody was anxious to enter the new gym. Through a narrow door, it was as if you didn't have to walk since the crowd carried you into the gym. Unfortunately, due to a flu epidemic in the community, there was no feast prepared for the event. However, cake and coffee was served to the public and, without a doubt, Puvirnituq was just as grateful to receive and own a new facility that will occupy the youth and all ages alike for its special events, including the popular Snow Festival it holds every spring.

The two facilities were funded by Makivik and were built from ground up by the construction company Chartel, the same company that built the two story Makivik building in Kuujjuaq, in 1996. Although we are in the modern days, the new gyms are a gateway to pursue the cultural aspect of Nunavik. Activities, games, singing and dancing shall continue: let the games begin.

(Makivik Magazine, Winter 2001, page 9)

Avataq Venture in the Business World with Its Tisanes
By Isabelle Dubois

The Avataq Cultural Institute was created in 1980 with a mandate to support, protect and promote the Inuit culture. Since then, Avataq has undertaken important research projects in the fields of language, folklore, country foods and traditional medicine, to name just a few. In 1983, Avataq launched the Traditional Medicine Project, in response to a request from elders who wanted ancestral knowledge about traditional medicines to be passed down to future generations. Information on traditional medicine was gathered from all the communities in Nunavik and a booklet was published in 1984 on how to heal cuts and bruises, relieve headaches, as well as the use of plants to make herbal teas.

When thinking of ways to generate funding, Avataq was looking for some kind of commercial venture that would bring in capital to finance its cultural activities. It was then that Avataq President Robbie Watt thought he could turn an idea he once had into a business opportunity: marketing traditional Inuit herbal teas. Robbie explains: "I was basically brought up by my grandmother, Daisy Watt, and grew up around elders who used plants for different purposes, one of them being herbal tea. When they would run out of tea from the Hudson Bay Company, they would gather plants and make their own. One day when I was out on the

land around my hometown, Kuujjuaq, I saw these plants and I thought this could be a possibility, but I forgot it for a little while. And then when I got into Avataq, I realized that there was an opportunity." Peter Abraham, an elder from Kuujjuaq, was then hired to do some research. It was decided that Qisirtuutaujak (Ground Juniper), Ukiurtatuq (Arctic Blend), Mamaittuqutik (Labrador tea), Paunngaqutik (Crowberry) and Arpiqutik (Cloudberry) would be gathered to make what would become Avataq's five blends of herbal tea.

In 1999, a pilot operation was launched, in which a very small amount of plants was collected to make samples of herbal teas that were given out to major organizations in the region and the communities as a way to test the product. People were struck by this idea of Robbie's. It was the first time that Inuit were taking advantage of their region's flora and traditional knowledge in a commercial way. Even Greenland was very impressed with the idea, which for them seemed as valuable as gold.

In the summer of 2000, a larger but still limited commercial harvest was conducted again around Kuujjuaq, where the climate and geography is favourable to the growth of the plants used in herbal teas. Students were hired through KRG's summer employment program to harvest 550 kilograms of plants. These were then aired out for a day and dried for about a week under a tent, before they were shipped in bags to Montréal, where the tisanes were produced. Once bagged, the tea was brought back up North and distributed in different communities to complete a marketing survey and see what Inuit thought of the product. Over 200 responses were received. Elders especially expressed their appreciation for the tisanes, as it reminded them of being out on the land. Some nursing stations in Nunavik and transit houses in the south were so delighted with the tisanes and the beneficial effect they have on the patients' morale that they requested to carry them in their facilities.

Following the survey, a commercial look to the product was developed. Northern Delights, as it is now called, was finally available for sale this past winter up North, primarily in Kuujjuaq, through Newviq'vi. The FCNQ has also shown interest in carrying the product in the different Co-op stores across Nunavik. Travelers to the North have also been targeted through advertisements in *Above & Beyond*, a magazine featured on all First Air flights. While samples were given out to different organizations and government offices involved with the North, the new product was also introduced on the market in the south, in some hotels and restaurants, as well as in some commercial outlets.

Since its introduction on the market, tisane sales have increased in a way that was never expected: orders are now often done by the case and some retailers sell close to $1,000 in tea bags each month! The tea is now sold through Avataq Corporation, a wholly owned subsidiary of the Cultural Institute created for its commercial activities. The secret recipes for these particular herbal teas belong to Avataq, and are protected under a license. The product was recently exposed on the international market at a food and

beverage trade show, SIAL, in Montréal last March, where buyers from all over the world are present. "The response was very positive," says Bruno Pilozzi, a consultant hired by Avataq for this specific project, "but although there are plans to go international, we have to build our inventories first to meet the demand."

As a matter of fact, 1.5 gram of each herb is needed per tea bag. Harvesting will take place in five communities this summer: Kuujjuaq, Kangiqsualujjuaq, Kuujjuaraapik, Umiujaq and Inukjuak. Due to their southern most location, these communities are more abundant in plants. The summer also lasts longer, which provides more time for collection, just to meet the current demand, 750 kilograms of fresh herbs will have to be collected per community. A manager has been hired in each community, whom will be responsible for showing the people the plants and how to collect them without creating any damage to the flora. The objective is to make these communities self-sufficient so that next year they can start the collection on their own. The harvesters are not paid on a salary basis but by the quantity they bring in. This enables them to do it on their own free time, while out on the land or at camp. Collection of the herbs will eventually be done in all communities of Nunavik and Avataq hopes that it will lead to small businesses being created.

Once the herbs are dried, they are sent to Transherb in Montréal where they are blended with other ingredients before packaging takes place. Research was done by chemists on how the medicinal extracts present in the herbs could be preserved and enhanced. For instance, ground Juniper, which was traditionally boiled and drunk for colds and lung ailments, now contains a little bit of echinacea, also known for its positive effect on colds. Other ingredients such as juniper berries and lemongrass have been added to make the taste less bitter. However, no artificial flavour, sugar, preservation agent or caffeine are added to the natural blend. Hence, each blend of Northern Delights tisanes has kept its medicinal properties.

According to Robbie Watt: "Ground Juniper was a plant that was used by the mid-wives for women who had just given birth. Some women lose a lot of blood when they deliver a baby. Ground juniper contains a lot of iron, which helps to strengthen and rebuild blood. Boiled, it can also be drunk to sooth bladder ailments and kidney pain.

Our kidneys are filters that clean out our whole system, but sometimes the channels are clogged up. Ground Juniper helps cleaning up your kidneys by making urine more clear."

Labrador tea could be seen as something to replace Tylenol with, for headache and pain relief. It can also help with breathing problems and to stop bleeding.

The Arctic Blend, which contains all parts of the stem, leaves and flowers of the Ukiurtatuq, can be used to counter the effects of stomach aches and general sickness.

Both the leaves of the Cloudberry plant and the Crowberry herb were traditionally boiled and used to settle an upset stomach and sooth the digestive system. The Cloudberry tea can also help with kidney and general ailments.

Both infusions produce a very fruity good tasting tea. "As iced tea, it's almost like Coolaid," says Robbie, who enjoys drinking it cold as a refreshment on a hot summer day.

(Makivik Magazine, Summer 2001, page 38)

Funds to Northern Québec

The Solidarity Fund QFL fulfills several missions, one of which is to invest in Québec's businesses and to provide them with technical support to enhance their development. By investing in small and medium enterprises, the 17 regional solidarity funds contribute to the creation and sustenance of jobs throughout the province. The Solidarity Fund QFL has recently announced an increase of $6 million to the capital of its regional fund in Northern Québec, bringing the total investment in this five year old regional fund to $12 million. "We are pleased with the Northern Québec Regional Fund's performance to date and are therefore increasing its budget by $6 million to enable it to continue supporting job creation and the emergence of solid business projects," stated the Solidarity Fund QFL President and Chief Executive, Mr. Pierre Genest. Since its inception in 1997, the Northern Québec Solidarity Fund has partnered with 15 companies in the region, including Katinniq Transport and Arctic Consultants. Project investments total over $23 million and have created or maintained 145 jobs. As of June 30, 2002, this regional fund's partner companies employed 121 people.

"Decisions in the region are made by people of the region, for the well-being of the region," noted Mr. Genest. Each region has its own board of directors, responsible to decide where to allocate their funds. Under the direction of Mr. Claude Ladouceur, the Northern Québec

Solidarity Fund Board of Directors is composed of Creé members from the James Bay area, while Jean Dupuis represents Nunavik with another member to be appointed by KRDC. The regional fund's priority is to help develop tourism, communications and transport industries, and to promote regional natural resources. For more information, contact the Northern Québec Solidarity Fund QFL in Chibougameau at (418) 748-8180, by fax at (418) 748-7121, or by e-mail at cladouceur@ndq.fondsreg.com. You may also log onto the Solidarity Fund QFL's Web site, at www.fondsftq.com

(Makivik Magazine, Fall 2002, page 46)

Allocation of Sanarrutik Monies

Following the signing of Sanarrutik, our tool for economic development in Nunavik, a joint committee of eight people has been set up to oversee its implementation. This group holds four people from the Government of Québec, two from Kativik Regional Government, and Treasurer Anthony Ittoshat and lawyers Bern Pennee and Sam Silverstone who represent Makivik. Though the joint coordinating committee has not had the opportunity to meet, the provisions outlined in Sanarrutik continue to develop.

Less then three months after the signing of Sanarrutik in Tasiujaq last April 9th, the Kativik Regional Government (KRG) entered into four other agreements. One is to pave the community roads signed with the Québec Ministry of Transport, two others will improve police services and build police stations signed with Public Security Québec, and another is for the creation of five provincial parks. Some $18 million for the creation of provincial parks including Pingualuit Park have been distributed as promised and plans continue to build Pingualuit as a tourist attraction (where the Nunavik Crater holds some of the earth's purest water). As well, KRG continues negotiations for a block funding arrangement as agreed upon in Sanarrutik. These events have meant a remarkably busy period for the KRG.

When Nunavik and the Québec government representatives met in June to plan the construction of an Inuksuk in Québec City, the first cheque was presented to Makivik President Pita Aatami and KRG Chairman Johnny Adams. Seven million dollars was designated for community and economic development, and shared between KRG and Makivik as provided for in Sanarrutik. From the first $7 million, KRG and Makivik each received $2 million. Another $3 million is distributed to various other Nunavik organizations.

The following organizations will be receiving such allocations for the next 24 years. Here are their allotments from the community and economic development funds received by Makivik, which has been distributed this year: The Landholding Corporations received $1.5 million; Anguvigaq Hunting, Fishing, and Trapping Association(HFTA) received $300,000 plus $50,000 for their work on the stream enhancement; Saputiit Youth Association received $300,000; Avataq Cultural Institute received $500,000; and Taqramiut Nipingat Incorporated received $300,000.

(Makivik Magazine, Winter 2002/2003, page 63)

Nunavik Creations Update

Nunavik Creations has opened four sewing centres in Nunavik; one each in Inukjuak, Salluit, Kangirsuk and Kuujjuaq. Nunavik Creations is using the sewing workshops built by Makivik Corporation in the first three communities. In Kuujjuaq, Nunavik Creations is using the women's auxiliary building as a sewing centre. There are two seamstresses working in each centre as well as a quality control manager. The seamstresses are using industrial sewing machines and fur sewing machines provided by Makivik Corporation.

The seamstresses have been hired to make clothing for the general public and fill special orders from organizations in the North and the south. Vickie Okpik from Makivik Corporation is the designer for Nunavik Creations. Dyed sealskins and furs are used extensively in the designs. To order your garment you need to go to the centre where the sewer will take your measurements while you choose the design and colours of fabric and fur.

Nunavik Creations has also opened a store in the old Nunavik Tourism Association offices in Kuujjuaq. The store sells a mix of products made by people from different communities as well as Nunavik Creations designs. All of these same products are sold on the website *nunavikcreations.com*.

Nunavik Creations presented their designs at a fashion show held in Québec City as part of the ceremonies for the Inukshuk unveiling and received rave reviews as well as orders for our products. Our collection of sealskin hand-bags, belts and ties is also very popular.

The goal of this project is to bring jobs to the communities as well as supplemental income from selling products on the internet. The hope is that with greater demand for the products, more seamstresses can be hired in the communities.

(Makivik Magazine, Winter 2002/2003, page 65)

"Hey! Wait for me!"

Showcasing Northern Business in Ottawa

The Labrador and the Baffin Regional chambers of commerce initiated the Northern Lights Trade Show, which was held at the Ottawa Congress Centre this past January 30th to February 2nd. After some executive deliberations, and since Nunavik has no chamber of commerce, Makivik's Economic Development Department then led the corporation into becoming a partner in the multi-industry venture. The overall planning took 18 months but Makivik's involvement began in June of 2007.

Ottawa was chosen as a gateway city to the North, which was an obvious choice due to the high traffic of various agencies through the city. Makivik subsidiaries First Air and Air Inuit also provided sponsorship, along with other northern corporate and government entities.

Planning committees were established for the various functions such as arts and culture presentations, musical performers, scheduling, floor plans and designs.

The task of organizing the event, in itself, was an opportunity for many people from all three northern regions to work together for this common need to educate southern based suppliers and consumers of what the North has to offer in terms of business and the economy.

When Makivik made its financial contribution, the FCNQ and the KRG were very quick to become involved and this made for very significant Nunavik participation of mostly private businesses. The mining industry was repre-

sented by some Nunavimmiut and tourism was also promoted through the Nunavik Tourism Association. Smaller businesses were represented thanks to financial assistance from the KRG.

The conference sessions offered a northern perspective in which Nunavik was well represented. Johnny Adams was master of ceremonies on the first day and later as a moderator of Cultural Industries and Tourism. He emphasized that the North these days has the "undivided attention of the world" particularly due to the many effects of climate change so northerners have an opportunity to take advantage of this world attention economically. Pita Aatami gave a welcome speech during the first night as well, and George Berthe later spoke on Cruise Ship Development during a conference session. The president of ITK, Mary Simon, also made the speech she had been presenting to audiences during her tour across Canada, "Inuit and the Canadian Arctic: Sovereignty Begins at Home."

Many Nunavik exhibitors and participants were unable to make it to Ottawa because the weather was too poor for travelling but this did not diminish the overall success of the show. It gave leaders from the three regions time to meet in an informal manner and for other networking to take place among those involved in building Canada's northern economy. Attracting a large amount of media attention to the Ottawa event was General Rick Hillier, Canada's Chief of Defence Staff. While many hoped he would speak about military initiatives in the North, General Hillier's speech focussed mainly on the role of the Canadian Forces in Afghanistan.

The three days of northern hospitality, northern entertainment and displays of rich northern art and culture culminated in a gala supper at the National Museum of Civilization with musical and comic performers, a fashion show, and an auction of art pieces from which the proceeds went to the homeless.

A follow-up survey was being done at the time of writing to determine the level of satisfaction and provide information as to whether this trade show will be repeated in the future.

(Makivik Magazine, Spring 2008, page 30)

Inuit Construction Company

At the general meeting of the Makivik Corporation in Payne Bay, the establishment of a new Inuit construction company in Northern Québec was discussed. This construction company, which will be called KIGIAK, originally planned to have it's main operation in Great Whale River with a sub-operation in Fort Chimo. But after a Makivik board meeting, the construction company will start operation this summer in Fort Chimo. Approximately 35 people from Northern Québec will be hired to put up an apartment block, 3 houses for the staff, and a warehouse. They will also add a second story to the Makivik office in Fort Chimo this summer. There are also other contracts planned for the construction company.

A new Inuit construction company is to be established in Fort Chimo to serve Northern Québec.

(Atuaqnik, April 1979, page 9)

New Nursing Stations for Aupaluk and Akulivik this Summer

Both Aupaluk and Akulivik will get proper nursing stations built this summer, announced the Kativik Board of Health and Social Services. Each station will come equipped with two nurses.

Aside from the improved health services both settlements will receive, the construction of nursing stations now means that the government now fully recognizes Akulivik and Aupaluk as established communities. In the case of Aupuluk, this brings the added advantage of having the proper electrical service and generator installed this summer along with the construction of gas and oil stowage tanks.

The Kativik Board of Health and Social Services has announced that Aupaluk and Akulivik are recognized as established communities, and will receive proper nursing stations. Aupuluk will also have electrical services, generators, and gas and oil storage tanks installed.

(Atuaqnik, May 1979, page 5)

Problems with Tosiujak's Nursing Station Continues
By M. McGoldrick

The problems with Tasiujak (Leaf Bay) are made very interesting by a number of points.

First, the current nursing station is much too small, so small as to make it a fairly serious problem.

The second point is that just about everybody agrees that it is too small and that the present residence of the Québec agent in Tasiujak would be an improvement as a nursing station because of its larger size. In fact just about everybody agrees that a switch should be made, since both buildings belong to MTPA of the Québec Government. Agreement on this matter includes everyone directly affected such as the Québec Agent, the nurse, the community, and the Kativik Board of Health and Social Services (of the regional government).

Third point, the bureaucrats of SAGMAI in Québec City say no to any suggestion of a switch. Reasons given —sufficient room in current nursing station and the residence of the Québec agent needs the extra space for the lodging of transient Québec Government officials.

Last point—When it comes down to choice between providing an important service to a community, and maintaining their own bureaucracy, bureaucrats always choose the latter.

However, Paul Bussières of the Kativik Board of Health

and Social Services says that the current mix up is not entirely the fault of the Québec Government. He said that if the Tasiujak Health committee had pressured a bit more last year when it was time, their nursing station would have been put on the priority list for improvement which would have probably resulted in the construction of a new one this summer. In addition, he said that regardless of this, the Kativik Board of Health and Social Services should have been aware enough of the situation to have put the nursing station on the priority list by itself.

(Atuaqnik, May 1979, page 7)

Building Up Kigiak
By Moses Koneak

At the general meeting in Payne Bay, Makivik Corporation established a new Inuit Construction Company. This new company, which is called Kigiak, is well on it's way for it's first season of operation. Kigiak Construction Company has already 6 contracts this summer.

The contracts they will be doing are: 10 Makivik houses, 2nd floor to the Makivik office, a warehouse for the Ayapirviq Restaurant and Air Inuit in Kuujjuaq (Fort Chimo). They will also put up the TV and Radio Production Centre in Sugluk. In addition, Kigiak will build seven houses of their own, and a service centre for its operations.

According to Sam Stone, secretary for the company, they are investigating the possible use of experimental wind and solar power for their service centre.

Kigiak will have 20 Inuit employees which will be permanent, Out of the 20, they'll probably have trainees in trades such as plumbing, electrician, supervising, etc. seven experts will be brought up from the south for the starting of the projects. Kigiak has seasonal jobs for 125 people.

The construction company is also bringing up a cement making factory which will be portable by boat. They plan to use this machine in any major construction site in any community in Northern Québec. The cement factory will be able to produce cement as well as concrete blocks of various designs.

General Manager of Kigiak, Bryan Forrest says, "that the cement factory is the step in the direction of developing construction industry that will use northern resources." This could mean that northern construction projects will rely less and less on material that have to be shipped up from the south. In the long run this will save money and will mean more jobs in the North.

"Arctic Québec comes first," says Forrest, "because it's the home of the company." However, Kigiak is planning on stretching across NWT in the future. Already Kigiak had to turn down a contract in Clyde River because they just came out and had other contracts lined up.

(Atuaqnik, Summer 1979, page 9)

Fencing Off Kuujjuaq's Airport
By Michael McGoldrick

During August, the people of Kuujjuaq (Fort Chimo) noticed that the Ministry of Transport (MOT) is putting up a fence that separates the passenger area around the terminal building from the tarmac where the planes refuel and park.

Once this fence is closed up, it will also prevent people from using the range road, which runs for about 3 to 4 miles and is one of the community's favourite spots for riding, collecting good fresh drinking water and picnicking. In addition, the road also leads to some gravel pits that are used for town construction projects.

For these reasons, many people have been wondering when the fence is going to be closed up and what is going to happen. Good news. MOT says that they will not close up the fence until another road to the range is built. According to the Director of the MOT facilities in Kuujjuaq, Jacques Cardinal, this other road probably won't be built until next summer. Until then, MOT will continue putting up the fence, but will leave the gate open.

In the meantime, MOT plans to be more strict about people who carelessly cut across airport facilities to get to the range road. Jacques Cardinal says that at no time should unauthorized people go onto paved areas, and that when passing by the tarmac, people should be careful and keep a good eye on airplanes that are coming or going. He

points out that planes do not have brakes or a horn as do road vehicles. Also, when using the road along the airstrip to get to the range, people should stay as far as possible from the paved runway. Mr. Cardinal also recommends that people stop when a plane is landing or taking off. He explains that this will make the pilots realize that the people on their motorcycle or skidoo are aware that the plane is there. Some pilots are afraid that someone might cut across just as they land or take off. Mr. Cardinal says that he has already found people on the runway with their bikes when Nordair was making its final approach. He also gave the example that there have been cases of airplanes hitting skidoos and motorcycles in other airports in Canada.

In the future, all of these problems will be overcome once another access road is built which will allow people to get to the range road without passing along the runway. Last year MOT had actually started work on such a road which ran along the Koksoak River. But part of this road was washed out by the spring flood and MOT is not sure if they will try to finish it. Instead, MOT is thinking of joining the Stewart Lake road with the range road. But this would only be done next year if the project was accepted by the various other organizations in town and if there is enough equipment to build it.

Jacques Cardinal also told *Atuaqnik* that MOT has plans to move the airport radio facilities to a trailer that will be put behind the terminal building. This will make the airport operations safer because the radio man will have a clear view of both runways, a situation which does not exist now. It is not sure when the trailer will be brought in, but it will probably be next year. In addition, Mr. Cardinal said that they will be lengthening the paved tarmac area by about 250 feet. With this, it will easily extend in front of the Air Inuit hanger.

(Atuaqnik, October 1979, page 11)

Sammy Kudluk

Québec to KRG: Only 8 Houses for Taqramuit this Year

The severe housing shortage in Northern Québec may soon become a crisis this year when only 8 new houses will be built for the whole territory.

On April 21, officials of the Québec Government informed the Kativik Regional Government that they would only be able to provide 8 houses instead of the 50 houses they were suppose to guarantee. Québec said that they only have money to build four houses in Akulivik and four houses in Aupaluk. In addition, four houses in Tasiujuk (Leaf Bay) will be renovated. However, this means that all the other communities in Northern Québec will not be receiving any new housing this summer, and the plans for distributing the badly needed houses that was worked out by the Kativik Regional Government last January are now useless.

Originally, the Québec Government, through the Québec Housing Corporation (QHC), promised 60 houses for Northern Québec at a value of $3.6 million. Later, they said they could only guarantee 50 houses or less, and now this is down to 8. Meanwhile, the Kativik Regional Government estimates that a total of 389 houses would have to be built in order to meet the immediate needs of the population.

During the past few years, under the Northern Housing program with the Department of Northern Affairs,

Northern Québec had been receiving 30 to 36 houses a
year. However, responsibility for providing housing to the
territory was transferred to Québec.

The reason for the cut back in the number of houses is
not completely clear. It is known that the QHC submitted a budget to the Québec Treasury Board to build 50
houses at an expense of $92,000 each. However, the Trea-
sury Board turned down the request because the estimates
of the cost of the houses by the QHC was all wrong. Apparently, the QHC could not give accurate figures for the
construction and maintenance costs. Somehow the QHC
did manage to get some money from the Treasury Board
for the houses in Akulivik, Aupaluk, and Tasiujak because
housing in these communities was always the responsibility
of Québec.

In addition, a number of people in high positions have
suggested that there might be some other reasons behind
the small number of houses Northern Québec is to receive
this year. It has been said that the cuts could be the result
of recent complaints by the Inuit about their dissatisfaction
with the way Québec is going about implementing parts
of the Agreement. There is a problem—a transfer payment
of $8 million from the federal government to the prov-
ince because of a lack of consultation with northern bodies
such as the Kativik Regional Government. And of course,
the whole referendum question on the future of Northern
Québec and Québec could be affecting things.

Both Willie Makiuk, President of the Kativik Regional
Government, and Charlie Watt, President of the Makivik

Corporation, have indicated that these political problems could be connected with the fact that the communities will not be getting the houses they were supposed to.

One thing that is becoming apparent with the whole situation is that if the Kativik Regional Government had been handling the housing program from the beginning as they wanted to, the communities would probably be receiving the proper number of houses this year. Instead, the regional government was given a small role and a reduced budget, and told that the Québec Municipal Affairs and the QHC could handle the housing program for Northern Québec. But it is now evident that the QHC and Municipal Affairs were "trying to do a job in the North that they don't know how to do," and that Kativik should have been given the responsibility along with the necessary budgets to carry out their work.

Apparently, some Québec officials are now quietly saying that things had not gone as well as they had hoped with Municipal Affairs, and that in the future they will be more open with the regional government. Whether this means that that regional government will be receiving enough funds in the future to carry out all their responsibilities remains to be seen.

Whatever the case, QHC's failure to obtain enough money from the Treasury Board means that Inuit families will have to go without their proper homes this year.

(Atuaqnik, April/May 1980, page 6)

KRG to QHC: More Houses Please!
By Alec C. Gordon

The housing shortage in Northern Québec and the supply of electrical power in the communities were both major topics at a recent joint meeting of the Councillors of the Kativik Regional Government and representatives of all the community Councils.

It is the first year that the Québec Housing Corporation (QHC) is suppose to be providing housing for Northern Québec and there are already some serious problems. In addition, there is a dangerous situation that is growing because of improper maintenance of electric generators and systems in some communities.

Housing
There was a great deal of discussion on this topic at the meeting. The amount of money to be spent on housing this summer totals $3.6 million. With this amount the Québec Housing Corporation had promised 60 houses, but now only guarantees 50 houses or less. The Kativik Regional Government has estimated that a total of 339 houses have to be built in Northern Québec in order to meet the immediate needs of the population.

With the limited amount of money for housing projects this summer, the delegates of each community were, of course, not very satisfied with the situation. Because of the limited number, each community delegate had to fight for

every house they could get for their communities. Some ended up giving away a house to another community that needed it urgently. Nevertheless, each settlement could not get the exact amount of houses that they needed and will have to wait several years to receive all the houses they require. But by then, housing needs will probably greatly increase and they still will not be able to catch up.

The houses which the QHC will bring to the North for Inuit families, for the first time, are duplex models. The QHC thinks that it will be much cheaper to heat and build the houses. However, people in the North are not happy with what the QHC will be bringing, especially those in the smaller communities. They feared that duplex housing will create a lot of social problems, which they feel always happens when any number of people are grouped together in one place. Another thing that they don't like about the duplexes is that if the house burns down, two units would be lost. The bigger communities are not really happy with the duplex situation but did not complain too much because of the urgency of their housing needs.

The QHC has just recently started to work on the plans of the houses and time is running very short for getting everything done so that the houses can come up this summer. The regional government expects if there is absolutely no delay with QHC, the communities could expect to see some new housing projects this summer or fall, after the ship arrives with the supplies.

Number of homes (houses) to be distributed to each community:

George River	4
Kuujjuaq	8
Leaf Bay	4
Aupaluk	10
Payne Bay	2
Koartak	2
Wakeham Bay	2
Salluit	6
Ivujivik	2
Akulivik	4
Povungnituk	6
Inukjuak	8
Great Whale River	2

Number of houses required to meet the immediate needs of the population in the communities:

George River	10
Kuujjuaq	42
Leaf Bay	3
Aupaluk	7
Payne Bay	8
Koartak	7
Wakeham Bay	12
Salluit	38
Ivujivik	7

Akulivik	34
Povungnituk	45
Inukjuak	50
Great Whale River	34

(Figures provided by the Kativik Regional Government.)

Electricity

Another topic that was discussed was the supply of electricity in the communities. Most of the smaller communities wanted regular inspections of their generators by qualified electricians and proper maintenance of damaged power lines. Some communities said that their generators were not strong enough for the demand of electricity.

The community with the worse problems is Aupaluk. Last summer MTPA's electrician went to the community to install the power lines from the generator and to wire up a few of the houses, but did not complete some houses. Because of the uncompleted job, the people had to scrounge for their own wire and hook it up to their houses. The delegates from Aupaluk explained that even old scraps of Bell Canada wire was used to light up the houses. Some of the houses do not even have panel boxes for the electricity which has already caused much damage to their electrical appliances.

Because MTPA did not act fast enough when they promised they would complete the job, Aupaluk got tired of not having electricity and decided to do the job themselves. Unfortunately, the material they used was not proper and raises a very dangerous problem for the people. Already a house has burned down because of poor electrical conditions.

Generally, the delegates and councillors strongly criticized MTPA for being an organization that is always willing to do everything but never living up to their promises, or being a year late with carrying out its promises.

(Atuaqnik, February 1980, page 1)

"Wanna play ice soccer?"

Proposed Housing Program

The housing plan that was drawn up by the Kativik Regional Government called for the building of single family dwellings in Northern Québec.

During the five year period from 1981-1986 the report stated that a minimum of 440 units should be build. Also mentioned was a five year restoration program, which will be finalized at a later date.

Construction should be started in all communities by the first three years, with the possibility of completing the construction in the smaller communities in one construction effort.

The original allotment for units will not take into consideration homes destroyed by fire. Each year a review will be done in the villages where construction is taking place to verify which ones had fire losses. When possible a replacement unit shall be built as soon as possible after the loss. It is estimated that five units will be destroyed by fire a year.

Also discussed in the proposal were the methods of construction presently available. The method of stick building, which is presently in use is favored, but the practical aspects of pre-fabricated components have to be taken into consideration.

Local entrepreneurs are to be favored up to 15% when contracts are tendered.

Basic house designs are to remain traditional, taking into

consideration the northern climate. However, some variety in the interior and exterior of these units is planned.

Some of the requirements for these homes are:
- hot/cold running water
- forced hot air heating system
- grey/black water disposal system
- complete electrical system
- humidification system
- stove, refrigerator, freezer
- beds and kitchen furniture
- separate living room and kitchen
- exterior storage area

One of the long term goals is a private ownership incentive program, which is advantageous to both the people of the territory and the province of Québec. The more people can be encouraged to become directly involved in housing the more independent they will become from the various types of social housing programs.

This could only be done with the close co-operation between all involved parties on:
1) subsidies for fuel;
2) loan assistance at rates comparable to the south and;
3) technical assistance especially in the areas of maintenance.

(Makivik News, October 1980, page 6)

All Set for Inukjuaks Arena

All of the materials required to build the foundation and shell of Northern Québec's first arena are now sitting in Inukjuak for the winter. This undertaking is supported by Makivik's Community Development Fund—formerly the Unallocated Funds—as the first of two such projects foreseen in the short term. Proper adjustment of the works with the level of activity in the community next spring and concerns about the provincial government's involvement are now on top of the agenda.

Site Ready
Recent financial contributions were directed towards the community itself and to Avataq Cultural Institute. The municipality has prepared the access road to the construction site and applied the final layers of gravel for the road bedding. Ian Badgley of Avataq has taken care of the surveys needed to evaluate and protect any ancient site eventually affected by the circulation of heavy equipment.

Steps have been taken to ensure that the hydro line will be run to the arena site in time for the works to resume next spring. Terratech Inc. began drilling to test the soil and their preliminary conclusion is that the site is right on bedrock.

Government Support Sought

Bruno Pilozzi, Head of the Community and Economic Development Department, expressed his concern that a project manager should now handle the coming steps. With an increased financial support by Makivik to community development, his Department must now concentrate on properly initiating its new programs and leave the highly technical stages to the specialists.

Negotiations are underway between the provincial government and Makivik, represented by Minnie Grey, Third Vice-President and Jobie Epoo, Treasurer, for the complete financing of the Inukjuak arena. SAGMAI has appointed Jean-Paul Matte, involved with the Relocation of Kuujjuarapik Inuit to Umiujaq, to serve as a project coordinator, beginning in January.

(Makivik News, December 1986–January 1987, page 35)

Inukjuak Arena Completed: Nunavik's First Indoor Rink Ready for Freeze-up

History was made this month when Nunavik's first indoor hockey and ice skating arena was completed in Inukjuak.

This test project was built during the summer of 1987 by the Municipality of Inukjuak, with the supervision of Makivik's Community and Economic Development Department. Inukjuak was chosen by Kativik Regional Government as the site for the first arena because it is the largest community on the Hudson Bay coast.

It is estimated that about 1,500 young people from both Inukjuak and the neighbouring communities may be able to enjoy using the arena.

Multi-purpose design

The design of the arena allows it to be used as a natural ice skating rink during winter months, and as a community recreational and cultural centre during summertime. Space has been provided in the building for the construction of commercial and office space. These facilities may be built in the future by the Municipality of Inukjuak.

The total cost of the project amounted to approximately $1.2 million, and was entirely covered by Makivik. Kativik School Board provided materials for construction of the boards around the rink, while the Municipality of

Inukjuak loaned bulldozers and other equipment for site preparation.

The Municipality of Inukjuak was also responsible for recruiting 26 local Inuit for the actual construction. Four elders participated, and twenty two young people worked during the three months of the project. The oldest of these Inukjuak youth was 19 years old. All had been previously unskilled in construction work.

The arena was designed to be built easily, and did not require specialized manpower. Wood was chosen for the main structure because it is the most flexible material in northern conditions.

The experience of the Salluit community centre taught Makivik that a simple, reliable design was vital for the success of the arena project. Given that this test project may lead to construction of arenas in other Nunavik communities, all possible construction difficulties were minimized.

The Inukjuak Arena is now ready to be used. While the official opening ceremony will take place later in the winter or during early spring, the youth of the Hudson Bay coast are already sharpening their skates and taping their sticks for the first season of indoor ice in Northern Québec. Who knows how long we'll wait before we produce the first Inuit hockey star in the NHL?

(Makivik News, November 1987, page 5)

Partners in Construction Management

Makivik has entered into a partnership agreement with a Montréal area engineering firm to start a construction management company for Nunavik. The company, called Gestion Sapummiq Management Inc., is a joint venture between Makivik Corporation and Plante et Associés, engineers for the Inukjuak arena project.

Makivik's Community and Economic Development Department (CEDD) had acted as Project Manager for the construction of Inukjuak's arena. Because of recent changes to the mandate and staff of the CEDD, the department cannot continue providing management services to construction projects in Nunavik.

Developing Recreation Facilities

Sapummiq was legally formed in May 1989, and is owned equally by Makivik and Plante. It will be responsible for all construction projects involving Makivik, and will take charge of the money allocated by Makivik for developing recreation facilities in Nunavik. Sapummiq will act as Project Manager on behalf of the communities for those projects.

Sapummiq will help the communities decide what kind of facilities they want, prepare bids for engineering and architectural plans, make cost estimates, arrange and coordinate shipment of building materials, and organize the required labour.

Sapummiq will charge a percentage of the total project cost for its services, but contracting with Sapummiq is not expected to increase the final cost of any construction project. This is because these services are needed for every project, although the existing Nunavik organizations and communities have not been able to provide them.

Inuit Employment a Priority

The new community centre in Salluit is likely to be Sapummiq's first client project. They will also supervise the completion of Inukjuak's arena roof this summer. Whichever community is ready will be next on the list.

Makivik may earn revenues from Sapummiq's management work, but this is not its primary objective. The goal of the joint venture is to ensure that construction projects in Nunavik are well administered, and that local Inuit workers are given priority of employment. One of the most important reasons for creating Sapummiq is to guarantee that local labour will be hired on construction projects, and the new company will work towards training Inuit project managers for the future.

All construction projects in Nunavik are free to sign contracts with Sapummiq for its professional services.

(Makivik News, June 1989, page 15)

Inuit Workers Start an Association: Building a Construction Industry

An Inuit owned construction company may be established in Nunavik by the middle of 1991. A group of Inuit carpenters have expressed interest in starting the company once they get professional diplomas from the Québec Government in April.

The company would make it easier for Inuit carpenters to benefit from the growing number of building contracts in the territory, and may also encourage more young people to pursue careers in the building trades.

Qualified carpenters who join the proposed venture will invest ten percent of their salaries in start-up costs, but the company also plans to approach Nunavik's organizations for support. Informal talks have been held with Makivik, Kativik Regional Government, and Kativik School Board (KSB) about possible joint ventures but their participation has yet to be determined.

KSB has been training Inuit carpenters and woodworkers since 1988. Twenty one trainees passed their courses in Kuujjuaraapik in May 1990 and sixteen were chosen to build Salluit's community centre for Sapummiq Management Inc. this summer.

Eight of the Salluit builders are now erecting a women's shelter in Kuujjuaq—a steel structure costing about $225,000. The core group to start the Inuit construction company may come from this team. Provided that the workers show they are able to run a business within a budget, there is talk of the company getting a contract for renovations in Kuujjuaq worth $150,000.

KSB's René Pelletier has worked with these students from the beginning and is proud of them. Pelletier says it was hard for the students to be away from their homes for such a long time, but that this is something they will have to get used to in the construction industry.

But there were problems at the construction site too.

"It was like working in the 1950s," says Pelletier. "We didn't have any equipment and most times we had to manually transport material to the construction site." Luckily, there were no accidents on the Salluit project.

Some of the Inuit workers complained about shortages of materials and delays in getting paid. The workers were paid between $8 and $14 an hour, but management difficulties and delays caused cost overruns for labour on the project.

The Salluit project was intended as a learning experience for the Inuit construction trainees, but outside pressures dictated that the community centre be used for the Eastern Arctic Summer Festival even though the building was not yet complete. As a result, some minor damage was caused to the structure.

There were also problems with theft and vandalism. Says Pelletier: "Everybody in Salluit was taking a piece here and there. It's a miracle that the centre is standing today." Young people were seen throwing rocks at the building even before construction was finished.

There have been reports of drug and alcohol related problems with a few of the construction workers too.

While the Inuit construction workers were training in Kuujjuaraapik they developed the idea of starting their own construction workers' association. It has been difficult since then to get the original group together, but once their work in Kuujjuaq is completed a foundation meeting will be organized.

"In the past, Inuit were always hired only as unskilled labourers," says Johnny Elijasialuk, secretary of the Northern Inuit Builders Association. "Our goal now is to make sure that Inuit become qualified carpenters."

"Nunavik needs this association because it will keep all Inuit construction workers together," René Pelletier says. The Builders Association will be the first example of organized Inuit labour in Québec.

Vice President Mark T. Gordon and Makivik's coordinator for Community and Economic Development, Bruno Pilozzi, recently travelled through Nunavik with a building expert to inspect the new arenas and community centres. They saw that the facilities planned for this year were all ready in time for the winter holiday season.

Kangiqsualujjuaq, Tasiujaq, Aupaluk, Kangirsuk, Kangiqsujuaq, and Povungnituk now have hockey arenas. In Ivujivik, Akulivik, and Umiujaq recreation centres were built for all types of sports and community functions. The total cost of Makivik's recreation construction program, originally planned at $9.78 million, is now estimated to total $10.5 million.

$1 million for Kuujjuaraapik

Kuujjuaq and Kuujjuaraapik are now the only communities where Makivik has yet to build recreation facilities. In Kuujjuaq, Kuujjuamiut Inc. is planning a multi-million dollar recreation complex with money from the Kuujjuaq (1988) Agreement. Sapummiq, Makivik's construction management subsidiary, is expected to handle this project.

Kuujjuaarapik representative Charlie Kowcharlie appealed to Makivik's Board of Directors in October to help his community get the recreation centre they have been wanting for a long time.

"We have asked for this for six years," Kowcharlie said as he presented plans for a recreation centre estimated to cost $1.9 million. "We don't want to wait for the hydro project for this to go through."

"You want a double gymnasium," replied Mark T. Gordon. "We have set aside $1 million for that. We can start when your community is ready."

Although the grant for Kuujjuaraapik's centre covers half of their needs, the Board of Directors passed a resolution which will start construction next autumn.

"The extra $900,000 can come later on," says President Charlie Watt. "Kuujjuaraapik is well informed and prepared to continue with this project."

(Makivik News, January 1991, page 25)

New Rent Scale for 1996

The proposed changes to the way social housing is delivered, notably the increases in the rent scale, will have a potential impact on a wide spectrum of Nunavik residents. The new rent scale is to be based on the household income level. A transition period will be put into place until 25% of income becomes the amount of rent to pay.

Makivik News had the opportunity to interview Kativik Regional Government (KRG) Chairman Jean Dupuis and discuss the history and current state of the social housing file, and more specifically on the rent scale adjustments to take place in April 1996. KRG is the main organization in charge of the social housing file and has taken part in negotiations with the Canadian Mortgage and Housing Corporation (CMHC) and Société d'habitation du Québec (SHQ).

A transfer agreement was signed in 1981 between Québec and Canada on providing social housing in Nunavik. It was then that the SHQ took over the housing program from the federal government. This agreement also meant that existing houses of the Department of Indian Affairs, referred to then as the "housing park," became the responsibility of the SHQ. The inherited buildings were below standards and hence a priority to renovate and replace them went into effect. Shortly after the agreement was signed, Makivik and KRG started negotiations with the federal government on a federal-provincial "catchup" program which had been proposed by the federal Tate Report. One of the aims of these negotiations were to "settle a program for replacing and renovating houses being transferred from the federal governmen," according to Dupuis who was also involved in the issue then.

When SHQ became directly responsible for social housing in Nunavik, the Northwest Territories (NWT) already had access to private home ownership. The leadership in Nunavik at the time was enthusiastic about the changes stemming from the 1981 agreement because there would be a prospect for a home ownership market. There were efforts to ask SHQ to access CMHC private home ownership programs, however, Québec soon announced that there would be only one applicable program: social housing.

After the announcement was made that there would be only one housing program in Nunavik. KRG went to Ottawa to get information on private home ownership programs being applied for in the NWT and Labrador. Dupuis said the government's response was that "a nonprofit housing corporation would have to be created. We looked at what this meant and found out that we would not be able to afford it." The subsidy for maintaining and operating houses being provided by SHQ would have been dropped if such a corporation were to be formed at the time.

Since 1981, the rent formula in Nunavik has managed to remain different from the rest of Canada, despite pressures to have it conform with social housing programs in other jurisdictions. Nevertheless, 1996 will be the year in

which a transition phase will begin and result in Nunavik tenants having to pay the same percentage as social housing tenants in the rest of Canada.

Back in 1994, Kuujjuaq Mayor Johnny Adams and Jean Dupuis met with the President of SHQ, Mr. Jean-Paul Beaulieu. As Dupuis put it, "He had good news and bad news." The good news was that the construction program in Nunavik would continue until 1995. The bad news was that the CMHC was demanding an additional $800,000 from the Québec program, resulting in SHQ's need to perceive that additional amount through rent collection. This increase in the region's contribution is part of a cost-sharing agreement between Canada and Québec. SHQ has access to the federal government's construction programs and serves as the "executioner" of such programs for Nunavik. Hence, due to changes in the way Québec receives transfer payments from Canada, Nunavik would have to face changes in the rent scale for social housing. During that meeting with Mr. Beaulieu, the target date for the increase in rent levels was January 1, 1995.

The original target date mentioned at the meeting with Mr. Beaulieu, as Dupuis stated, "was not realistic and the majority would not be able to adjust overnight." After further discussion regarding the social and economic situation in Nunavik, SHQ agreed to put together a working group composed of technical people from KRG and SHQ. This group was mandated to study the different aspects of how the new rent increase would affect the people.

One of the main items in the terms of reference of the

working group was to evaluate the capacity to pay. This work involved Makivik participation in terms of providing information on taxation returns. The documents were used without using peoples names and enabled the group to identify particular households and their capacity to pay.

As the working group progressed, the plan to change the rent formula in such a short time before an analysis and social impact evaluation was seen by Nunavik leaders as very unfair. The social impact evaluation was deemed as very necessary especially since there are hardly any housing alternatives due to there being only one existing housing program. Therefore, the working group also noted that there should be alternatives provided prior to the full operation of the rent formula.

Everybody agreed on these issues and a decision was reached to have "simulations" in the communities of Nunavik. These simulations were to take place in different regions and in different sizes of communities, according to Dupuis, "to get a good overview."

An important decision was also reached directly pertaining to the population of Nunavik. An information tour will be conducted by KRG starting in late June until August. 1995. The results of this tour would be ready by fall and the analysis of them are to take place in October.

Dupuis also stated that, "some civil servants respect the Inuit culture and traditions, but some have no respect at all and refer to the lifestyle in Nunavik as a 'luxury.'" Despite the lack of understanding in some cases, Jean added that the southern decision makers have only recently arrived at

a better understanding of the economic and social situation in Nunavik.

Despite the original target date for the launch of the new rent scale (January 1995), a transition phase will be incorporated in the program development. This transition "will be between 3 to 5 years." In other words, the 25% level of rent pay from the gross revenue of a household would be in full effect only after a few years.

When the new formula is imposed, tenants will have to go to their housing authority office and show their previous year earnings along with their T-4 slips and other income tax return information in order to receive a specific rent formula for the coming year. The formulation of rent pay is expected to consider specifics such as job changes and status.

At the time of the interview, Dupuis stated, "the formula for additional wage earners in a household and the like is still not at hand." This means that there will be different ways of calculating the actual rent amount of each particular household.

According to the structure of the new rent scale, old age pensioners, retired people and welfare recipients will pay less under the new system. Other groups that may face lower rent levels or very low rent pay will be the seasonal workers earning less than $20,000 annually.

Dupuis also mentioned that there will be a maximum rent imposed before alternatives are in place besides the single social housing program in Nunavik. A maximum amount is still at the discussion level and will be part of the transition period. This consideration reflects the avoidance of penalizing the higher wage earners too much, especially before alternatives such as a private home market are available.

The highest impact of the new rent levels is expected to be on the middle wage earners. Dupuis said, "The hardest hit will be the ones making between $25,000 and $50,000 annually." According to the negotiations on this file, the reasoning of the government is to avoid penalizing the lower wage earners when the higher wage earners can afford something more than social housing.

In the long run, wage earners might be affected in several ways by the new rent scale. One concrete prospect is the decline of purchasing power in the community due to higher amounts of money to pay for rent. This decline in consumer spending may affect the local businesses.

KRG is expected to be affected significantly by the imposition of the new rent scale too. As Dupuis put it, "KRG will have the burden of providing extra training to Secretary-Treasurers and Housing Managers." This training will be necessary because the rent pay will be formulated in a new way and follow-ups will be necessary throughout the process. Housing Managers are also expected to be closer to applying pressure to the people who get entangled in rent arrears.

A part of the transition phase and proposed changes to social housing in Nunavik is the pilot project for a home ownership program taking place in Kuujjuaq this summer.

This community was chosen for technical support and followup reasons. The objective of this project is to provide alternatives to social housing by the time the new scale is in full effect. Dupuis said, "Nine people are in this project and went through an evaluation process with KRG, SHQ and the bank." One immediate effect is that these people will be liberated from the waiting list.

Dupuis stated, "If we see success stories, we will be able to negotiate with Canada and Québec for a more permanent project immediately." It is expected that, by October or November, 1995, such success stories will materialize and therefore a point will have been made that people want to invest and that the waiting list and overcrowding problems could be alleviated.

The regular (and last) SHQ construction program will take place this summer and will mark the end of the federal commitment to social housing construction in Nunavik. This continuation was the result of the review of the 1981 transfer agreement by the governments, KRG, Makivik, and Senator Charlie Watt. The construction program for new houses or renovation will take place in the following communities: Kuujjuaq; Tasiujaq; Quartaq; Salluit: Puvirnituq; and Kuujjuaraapik.

(Makivik News, Summer 1995, page 27)

A Prize Contract for Nunavik
By Bob Mesher

The rain and swarms of mosquitoes at the Halutik gravel pit near Kuujjuaq on August 10th were not severe enough to drown out a ceremonial rock dumping there. The official performance commenced phase one of a two phase project to restore the paved aircraft maneuvering areas at the Kuujjuaq airport.

A group of dignitaries and their colleagues, including Gilbert Normand, Secretary of State (Agriculture and AgriFood/Fisheries and Oceans), Guy Saint Julien, MP for Abitibi-James Bay-Nunavik, Michael Gordon, Mayor of Kuujjuaq, Johnny Adams, Vice-President of KRG, and Louie Pomerleau, Manager of Halutik Fuel drove out to the site following a speech presentation at the Kuujjuaq Inn to start off the project.

Grandly announced by Mr. Normand on behalf of Canada Transport Minister David Collenette, the more than $1.5 million contract to manufacture crushed stone aggregate for the airport upgrade has been awarded to Halutik Fuel Inc., a subsidiary company of Makivik Corporation.

According to Guy Saint Julien, another stone crushing company located in the Lac Saint Jean area of Québec objected to the contract being awarded to Halutik Fuel, saying they could provide the aggregate from the south, and ship it up to Kuujjuaq. The federal MP says he found that plan unacceptable, and that the contract was to be awarded

locally instead.

"This was a heartening piece of good news which I hope will be more of a standard way of doing business," said Makivik President Zebedee Nungak following the announcement, "Considering that traditionally such contracts are usually awarded to outside companies and contractors that are not residents of Nunavik, I think this is a fine example of how contracts such as this can benefit an entity that exists within our territory. The Halutik Fuel Project should be the very model of how such things should be run, because what we normally see are contracts being awarded to outsiders, with all the benefits of such a contract going back out of the territory."

Mayor Gordon also expressed his gratitude to Transport Canada for the airport improvements, explaining the urgent need for a runway upgrade since the Kuujjuaq facility has not been overhauled since the 1960s. "Perhaps you noticed the cracks (in the tarmac)," he said to the Ministers who had arrived by plane, "We have been crack filling for the past two years but this just doesn't cut it anymore... (The contract) is also good for local employment."

"Without the Transport Canada contract," says Louie Pomerleau, "Halutik Fuel would have had to lay off some of their employees. Their main revenue source had previously been from serving as an agent for Shell Canada. Now Halutik can offer more work to their present employees, and has a chance to hire others." Pomerleau hopes the project will also provide the Makivik subsidiary an opportunity to expand into other interests. "This is good news because it means more revenue," he says.

At a cost of nearly $1 million, Halutik purchased a brand new loader and truck, both made by Caterpillar, last summer. The loader is equipped with a five and a half cubic-metre bucket, especially designed to work in rocks. Their new truck carries a payload of 30 tons. Both pieces of equipment are of the latest technology and comfort features for the operator. Halutik will be blasting rock to feed the crusher, set up in a quarry west of the airport facilities. Once the rock is crushed into gravel, it has to be hauled to a Transport Canada stockpile site near the runway. The stone will serve as a granular sub-base for the runway, and will be an ingredient in the new runway pavement.

Mr. Pomerleau explains that the new loader and truck, like other pieces of heavy equipment already owned by Halutik, may be routinely rented out for various other projects as well.

While the Kuujjuaq Airport remains the property of Transport Canada, it has been two years since the federal government and KRG signed an agreement to transfer management of the airport to local interests.

During the ceremony at the Kuujjuaq Inn, Normand mentioned it was his second visit to Kuujjuaq—the first trip as a sports fisherman. "I am very pleased that the Kuujjuaq project is underway. In addition to stimulating local employment, the airport improvement project will help to preserve the safety and efficiency of the facility," he said,

While stone crushing officially began on August 10, it will continue until October 1998. It will start again in June

1999 and terminate in October 1999. The two phases of the Kuujjuaq Airport improvement project to restore the paved aircraft is estimated at a cost of nearly $10 million.

Halutik loader operator Jean-Guy Briere instructed Gilbert Normand as he officially dumped the first load of rock into the crusher, while Guy Saint Julien sat in the cab of the powerful new "Cat" beside him. Many more buckets of rock will be dumped into the Halutik crusher before the airport improvements are complete. Beyond fulfilling the necessity to overhaul the Kuujjuaq runway, however, the project also provides Nunavik an important opportunity to demonstrate that the expertise and capability already exists within the region to manage such contracts.

(Makivik Magazine, Fall 1998, page 29)

Kuujjuaq Airstrip Shut-Down Averted

What would have been a costly shutdown of the Kuu-jjuaq asphalt airstrip during the summer months of 2000 and 2001 has been avoided. The federal transport department had proposed to shut down the main airstrip for repairs from July 2000 to September 2000, and again from July 2001 to September 2001. Instead, it will spend an additional $2 million to allow jet service to continue while it repairs the main 6,000 foot asphalt runway and lights. A total of $13 million will be spent to upgrade the airstrips.

A coalition of Kuujjuaq businesses to oppose the way in which the federal transport department planned to do the repairs. Shutting down the airstrip for the four crucial summer months would have crippled the tourism industry, and the vital transportation link to the Ungava coast. Transport Canada argued that it would have to spend $3.5 million to upgrade an existing gravel runway to maintain full 727 jet service. It was proposing rerouting passengers and cargo via La Grande, which would have had a considerable impact on travel time, and cost.

This issue was raised during a presentation made to the Standing Committee on Aboriginal Affairs in November 1998. During meetings held with the Canadian Minister of Transport David Collenette in early February 1999, a solution was found to upgrade the 5,400 foot gravel airstrip to allow a Boeing 737 to continue operations during the summer months. The work to upgrade the gravel runway will take place in the summer of 1999.

Makivik President Pita Aatami says there will still be added costs incurred with this solution, and that he will continue to seek a subsidy for First Air to deal with the estimated $1.3 million additional costs resulting from the use of a smaller jet.

(Makivik Magazine, Spring 1999, page 31)

Sammy Kudluk

Progress on Social Housing

There is some good news for Inuit hoping for new houses. An agreement has been reached with the governments of Canada and Québec for the construction of approximately 40 new housing units during the 1999 summer construction season. The federal government will contribute $5 million to the project, to be matched by Québec. It's a one year emergency funding package.

The new housing units will be built in the communities of Aupaluk, Kuujjuaq, Salluit, and Tasiujaq. The communities were selected by the Société d'habitation du Québec (SHQ), which will be renovating other homes there this summer.

Makivik and KRG leaders met with both Canadian and Québec ministers responsible for native affairs from January to March to formally discuss the issue of social housing. The Dispute Resolution Mechanism of the James Bay and Northern Québec Implementation Agreement was convened for the first time to clarify government housing responsibilities. No new social housing had been built in Nunavik since the summer of 1995.

Nunavik leaders told a Parliamentary Standing Committee in Ottawa on November 19th that there was an immediate need for 425 social housing units throughout Nunavik. The 40 units built during the summer and fall of 1999 will be a start to alleviate the problem.

Makivik, and the Government of Canada, agreed to

continue using the dispute resolution mechanism process to ensure a long term housing program for Nunavik.

(Makivik Magazine, Spring 1999, page 35)

Construction Begins: Kangiqsualujjuaq is First to See Work on Marine Infrastructures

After nearly two decades of negotiations with governments for the construction of marine infrastructures in the Nunavik communities, Kangiqsualujjuaq is the first to see any actual construction activity, which got underway last May 17th. Funding for the program in part was secured in June 1998 following the signing of a $30 million agreement with the federal government.

Makivik employed O'Neil Léger as the Project Manager. He brings not only technical experience to the project but also a knowledge of Nunavik, having worked at the Raglan Mine site for three years, as well as having managed the construction of the recreation centre in Inukjuak last summer on behalf of Laval Fortin.

Once completed the project has been designed to improve navigation safety conditions and access to water for residents of Kangiqsualujjuaq. The project also brings other spin-off benefits to the region. The importance of creating local employment and training opportunities has been a key aspect of the plan from inception. O'Neil Léger says although a few experienced technicians will be required to oversee particular aspects of rock blasting and crushing, as well as excavator operations, most workers such as mechanics, heavy equipment operators, kitchen staff and general labourers are Inuit. Conscientious work habits and

safety remain at the forefront during the season.

The Inuit employees at the project, as of June 5,1999 are; from Kangiqsualujjuaq: David Emudluk, Mathew Etok, Kitty Seguin, Molly Emudluk, Sem Tuglavina, Henry Ittulak, Bobby Assevak, and Penina Mae Etok; from Inukjuak: Josie Echalook; and from Kuujjuaraapik: Gilbert Weetaltuk.

A heavy equipment course is also taking place parallel to the construction project under the direction of the Kativik School Board and Kativik Regional Government, with six Inuit enrolled in the course.

The heavy equipment trainees at the site are; from Kangiqsualujjuaq: Joe Willie Etok, Danny Snowball and Jacko Jararuse; from Quaqtaq: Alik Aloupa and Paul Tukkiapik; and from Tasiujaq: Vallee Nayome.

No drugs or alcohol are allowed on site, and employees are expected to be on the job from 7 a.m. to 6 p.m., six days per week.

Another important benefit for Kangiqsualujjuaq is that, while the rock crusher is set up there, gravel will be produced for a number of other projects including the resurfacing of the airstrip, construction of the new school, construction and maintenance of municipal roads, and the relocation and construction of housing units and other buildings. This gravel will be sold to the local Qiniqtiq Landholding Corporation at cost, who will then make it available to the entities who require it.

The 1999 marine infrastructure project in Kangiqsualujjuaq is scheduled to be finished by the middle of September. Once the work is complete it will be handed over to the community. The heavy equipment is then expected to be shipped on the last sealift this fall to Quaqtaq for use during the 2000 construction season.

The Marine Infrastructure Program is overseen by a joint Makivik/Kativik Regional Government management committee as represented by Johnny Adams, Jean Dupuis, Pita Aatami, Johnny Peters, Watson Fournier, Michael Barrett and Eileen Klinkig.

Components of the project

(From Eileen Klinkig) Components of the project this summer include a main breakwater at Akllasakallak Cove, a beach access in Akllasakallak Cove, an access road to the main breakwater, a second breakwater in front of the community, and a beach and channel clearing in the bay. The main break water a second breakwater in front of the community, and a beach and channel clearing in the bay.

The main breakwater

In order to provide better access to the water, a new stone breakwater will be constructed in Akilasakallak Cove. The length of this structure will be 160 metres and the average height is 6.5 metres.

This structure is built of different sizes and shapes of stone, placed in layers of core material and armour stone. The sides of the breakwater will have a slope of 66% and the stone sizes are designed so that the structure will resist expected wave and ice action. Weight and size dimensions of armour stones will be 1,000 to 3,000 kilograms, for an average dimension of between 0.8 and 1.2 metres.

A hydraulic excavator will be used to place the armour layers. The estimate of stone required to build this breakwater is 24,000 m³ total. A quarry will be open on site to extract the required material for construction.

The beach access ramp

The protected beach will be accessible from the road by way of a stone and gravel ramp 20 metres wide at the road intersection narrowing to 10 metres wide at the lower water mark. The ramp is 55 metres long with a slope of 10%. This ramp down from the road will facilitate boat access to the water.

The access road

The road, which is about 500 metres long, runs along the Akilasakallak Cove above the high water level. It will link the village to the new marine service area. The rock on site will have to be leveled in order to build the road. As an extension to the road, there will also be a trail leading down to the traditional fishing grounds.

The second break water

A riprap extension will be built at a point in front of the village to protect the natural basin which serves, and will serve, as a haven for some of the boats. This stone structure will extend the current point by around 30 metres with an average height of 4.5 metres. The estimate of stone required to build this protection is 2,000 m³ total.

Beach clearing

Boulders will be removed from the beach and in the channel so that the designated area between the village and the main breakwater will be safer for navigation. The boulders will be used in the construction. The estimate of recuperated boulders is around 5,000 m³

Quantity of stone needed for construction

The quantity of stone needed to implement phase 1 of the Kangiqsualujjuaq marine infrastructure is estimated as follows: 11,000 m³ of armour stone; 6,000 m³ of filter layer stone; 16,000 m³ of quarry-run material; and 3,000 m³ of crushed stone; for a total estimate of 36,000 m³.

Quarries

The main quarry will be located at the main break-water. The rock is of sufficient quality to be used for the production of stones required in the infrastructure as core materials and armour stone.

In order to reopen the airport quarry, a certain amount of cleaning up will be necessary before production. All the material cleaned away can be used as back-fill for the construction of the access road. The estimate of material that would be transported by truck through the village is 1,000 m³, which represents about 100 truck loads.

The rock crusher will be installed at the airport quarry and will crush 3,000 m³ of stone on site, which will take about 18 days of work. All selected materials will be stock-piled.

(Makivik Magazine, Summer 1999, page 41)

Construction Boom in Nunavik
By Isabelis Dubois

Nunavik is growing and, with over half of the Inuit population under the age of 25, it is predicted to grow even more. According to the most recent data available from Statistics Canada, the population of Nunavik added up to 8,715 inhabitants in 1996. The current Inuit population is now close to 9,300, while the total Nunavik population today is about 10,000. (More precise data will be available in March 2002, when Statistics Canada will publish the results of the 2001 Population Census.) With a demographic growth rate higher than the rest of the province, the population of Nunavik is estimated to go as high as 11,052 within 5 years, to reach 12,498 in 10 years from now. With such figures, one can understand why Nunavik has seen many constructions bloom in its communities these past few years.

With a growing population, more houses are needed to accommodate everybody. Housing shortages are not something new in Nunavik, as it has always been an issue. In Nunavik, it is common to have two or three families living together. With an average of 4.3 individuals per family, over 10 people can sometime live under a same roof. According to Watson Fournier, Director General of the Kativik Municipal Housing Bureau (KMHB), Nunavik would need between 400 and 500 more houses to meet the demand for housing.

During the course of last year, Makivik Corporation established a Construction Division under the supervision of the President's Department, which was to implement a renewed Nunavik Housing Program with its already in place Marine Infrastructure Program. An agreement was then entered into with the federal and provincial governments, which provides funding of $10 million per year over a five year period, with a renewal clause for the construction of housing units in Nunavik. Following KMHB's recommendations and statistics data, the Kativik Regional Government Council is responsible for decisions on where the new houses will be built each year. Last year, 60 two bedroom units have been built in the following communities: Kuujjuaraapik, 9; Inukjuak, 18; Puvirnituq, 16; Ivujivik, 3; Kangiqsujuaq, 4; Quartaq, 5; and Kangiqsualujjuaq, 5. This summer, 17 one floor two bedroom duplexes are now under way: eight in Kuujjuaq; four in Kangirsuk; three in Akulivik; and two in Umiujaq. These duplexes will provide homes to 34 families.

The Construction Division works in close collaboration with KMHB, which acts as a proxy for SHQ, to ensure that the houses meet all of SHQ's required standards. Once the houses are built, they are transferred to KMHB for a nominal value, whom will then take care of renting the places and maintenance. The operating deficit resulting from low rent fees is subsidized by SHQ. The Construction Division works closely with the Manpower and Training Department of KRG to ensure that a maximum number of employment opportunities on the project are filled by

Inuit in order to promote the local economy. For the most part, apprentice carpenters with some experience are hired and on-the-job training is provided. With their apprentice card in hand, workers have to pay Union dues and report to the Comité de la Construction du Québec (CCQ) with the number of hours worked, as 6,000 hours of work experience are required to become an official carpenter. Theory courses could also be given eventually, during the winter, which would be followed by the CCQ exam.

With its decision to relocate up North, the Kativik School Board has also added to the number of houses being built. Ten two floor duplexes have been erected to accommodate KSB's Curriculum Development Department, which will be moving this summer to Kuujjuaq. More houses will be built in the following years to welcome the General Administration, the Education Services and the Adult Education Department to Kuujjuaq, as well as the Equipment Services and the Human Resources and Finance Department, to Kuujjuaraapik. The KSB Head Office will be located in the old Adult Ed building of Kuujjuaq, until October of this year, when a new building will be ready. The relocation should be complete within seven years from now. A larger population not only means more houses in the different communities of Nunavik, but also more facilities for its residents. Last year, Makivik funded the construction of two new recreation centers: one in Puvirnituq and one in Kangirsuk. Sewing and woodworking shops have also been built in Kangirsuk, Salluit and Inukjuak, to provide people with a working area. In the past few years, FM stations have also been built in nearly all communities of Nunavik. Following the successful completion of the marine infrastructure project in Kangiqsualujjuaq, Makivik also undertook the construction of such facilities in Quartaq last summer. Umiujaq and Kangiqsujuaq are next on the list for this summer, while Ivujivik and Kuujjuaq are scheduled for the summer of 2002.

As families grow, babies are born and there is an increased need for daycare services. Even though new Child Care Centres were built in nearly all communities of Nunavik in the past few years, it is not enough to meet the increasing demand. There are currently 657 subsidized places for pre-school children. However, the population for children under five years of age accounts for 1,448. As a result of the ever growing child population, new Child Care Centres will be built this year in Kuujjuaq, Puvirnituq and Quartaq, which should provide a total of 148 new places by January 2002. Tasiujaq should also get new daycare facilities next year. Makivik, who was previously committed to fund Child Care Centres until the year 2000, has agreed to contribute $100,000 to child care buildings over a four-year period, which will be built under KRG's Child Care Department.

Furthermore, Nunavik receives more and more visitors every year. To accommodate them, the FCNQ has invested in building three new hotels these past couple of years: a first one was built in Puvirnituq, another one in Inukjuak, and the most recent one in Kuujjuaq, last year. A new complex is also scheduled to be built in Kuujjuaq, to receive delegates for the Inuit Circumpolar Conference 2002. The facilities will then be used for different meetings and conferences, as well as to welcome performers in its auditorium during music festivals. The auditorium could eventually be used for movie projections.

(Makivik Magazine, Summer 2001, page 28)

Kids at the Avataq sponsored youth camp.

Government Grants Funds to the Construction of a Multi-purpose Centre in Kuujjuaq

Last November, Member of Parliament for Abitibi/Baie-James/Nunavik Mr. Guy St. Julien, announced that the Government of Canada intends to make a $1.5 million contribution towards the construction of the Kuujjuaq multipurpose centre, which will be provided by Canada Economic Development and the Department of Indian and Northern Affairs. "This project is of vital importance for the entire community of Nunavik. This infrastructure had become essential; its implementation will give Kuujjuaq a Cultural and Convention Centre of international stature which enable it, among other things, to host the next general meeting of the Inuit Circumpolar Conference, slated to be held in July 2002," stated the Honourable Martin Cauchon, Minister of National Revenue and Secretary of State responsible for Canada Economic Development. "The Cultural and Convention Centre project is an eloquent example of the Inuit community's vitality. It will not only serve as a catalyst for the economic development of Kuujjuaq, but will enable the community to become more self-sufficient," added the Honourable Robert Daniel Nault, Minister of Indian Affairs and Northern Development.

Member of National Assembly for Ungava Mr. Michel Letourneau also reiterated the Québec Government's commitment to contribute a little over $5 million for the construction of this multipurpose centre. Aside from the Ministère des Régions, which is contributing $2 million, four other Québec Government departments and agencies are providing financial support: the Secrétarait aux Affaires Autochtones ($600,000); the Ministère des Affaires Municipales et de la Métropole ($1,304,564); Tourism Québec ($500,000); and the Ministère de la Culture et des Communications ($729,852). "The construction of a cultural and convention centre will revitalize Kuujjuaq and unite the community. It also marks the concrete outcome of a fruitful partnership between Nunavik officials and the Québec Government," Mr. Letourneau noted. He also congratulated Johnny Adams, Chairman of the Kativik Regional Government, Michael Gordon, Mayor of Kuujjuaq, and Pita Aatami, President of the Makivik Corporation, for their commitment to this important project.

The multipurpose centre, now under construction, will bolster Kuujjuaq's position as an economic hub in Nunavik and foster job creation. As the venue for a number of major conventions, it is also expected to increase tourism for Nunavik as a whole. In addition to a 500 seat multipurpose auditorium, the centre will house various services such as the Kuujjuaq Municipal Office and the Nunavik Tourism Association's office. The centre will be designed to eventually include an interpretation centre that will house, in particular, the collection of Inuit artifacts stored at the Smithsonian Institute in Washington, D.C.

(Makivik Magazine, Winter/Spring 2002, page 7)

Breakwaters, Wharves, Houses and Jobs
By Eileen Klinkig

Since Makivik began construction of marine infra-structures for Nunavik communities in 1999, and social housing units in 2000, Phase I marine facilities have been built in eight communities, while complete marine projects are underway this summer in two communities and 186 housing units have been built throughout the region.

The 2003 building season was the first time in which communities have received both breakwaters and loading wharves constructed within the same year. These two communities are Kangirsuk and Salluit, and their wharves have been added as a direct benefit of The Sanarrutik Agreement, which was signed in the spring of 2002.

Prior to Sanarrutik, an agreement was signed in 1998 with the federal government which provided for $30 million over a 10 year period for the construction of the marine infrastructure facilities. In 2000, the federal government contributed an additional $5 million towards the purchase of a second set of construction equipment—for a total of $35 million. Back in 1996, the marine infrastructure program had been estimated at $88 million for all 14 Nunavik communities. However, as Makivik did not have sufficient funds to build in all communities, it was decided to develop the program in phases. To this end, Phase I aimed at improving access and safety to water for local residents and Phase II aimed at improving sealift operations. As

a result, from 1999 through to 2002, the Corporation built Phase I facilities in Kangiqsualujjuaq, Quaqtaq, Umiujaq, Kangiqsujuaq, Ivujivik and Kuujjuaq.

Providing additional necessary monies, Sanarrutik foresees matching funds received from the federal government up to a maximum of $44 million. As the marine infrastructure planning process takes up to two years prior to construction, Kangirsuk and Salluit were the first two communities slated for complete projects.

The project in Kangirsuk includes three breakwaters with two access ramps and service areas and a 12 metre by 16 metre concrete wharf equipped with a fixed hoist to unload cargo from small boats. In the process, a 2.2 kilometre road was built to the construction site from the quarry.

There are a number of reasons why three breakwaters were designed for Kangirsuk. One of the major determining factors in the design and length of the two breakwaters at Site 1 (i.e. the "Co-op side" of Kangirsuk) is the strong currents and the ice break-up in spring. These breakwaters could not be extended beyond the design without jeopardizing their stability, especially given the force of the ice during spring break-up. As a result, the sheltered area created by the two breakwaters is relatively small and will be quite congested, especially during sealift operations.

Beach clearing was also conducted in Kanik Cove, on the upper side of the community. The boulders from Kanik Cove have sharper edges than boulders found in most of our other beaches, which made them suitable for use in the construction of a breakwater at Kanik Cove. This third breakwater will ease congestion at Site 1.

Even during the pre-feasibility stage of the marine infrastructure program, the objectives of the program have been to design and build high quality facilities, while promoting economic development within the communities and providing employment for Inuit.

The use of readily available rock in the construction of the breakwaters rather than pre-fabricated cement blocks, caissons, or other materials shipped from the south allows for all of the work to take place in the North and thereby creating jobs for local and regional heavy equipment operators.

Although the design of each project changes, the construction process for these marine infrastructures is basically the same. From the workers point of view, what makes a project unique and significant are the people who build it.

In collaboration with the KRG and the KSB, the Makivik Construction Division has held a number of training programs over the years for heavy equipment operators and carpenters. With the growing population in Nunavik, infrastructure needs will continue to increase, resulting in more construction projects in the communities.

Therefore, the foreseen job opportunities for trained Inuit in Nunavik's construction industry is limitless. Needed expertise will include engineers, surveyors, heavy equipment operators, mechanics, concrete specialists, carpenters, electricians, plumbers, welders, environmental specialists, cooks and so on.

The transfer of knowledge to the next generation of construction workers is an invaluable benefit of this activity, as today's workers will certainly lead the way into future projects with sound knowledge based on his/her work experiences with Makivik Construction.

One challenge the employees face is being away from home for long periods of time. This is where team spirit and mutual support takes an increased importance.

It also helps to have the employees from Makivik's various construction crews working in the same groups for each project, as a healthy team spirit is essential to produce the amount of work that has to get done. The construction season in Nunavik is very short so there is very little margin for delays.

Safety is an utmost priority at all of Makivik's construction projects. Regular safety meetings are conducted to educate all workers on work safety. On-the-job experiences or observations are discussed at these meetings, giving everyone an opportunity to express their concerns.

The two bedroom duplexes that Makivik is building in Nunavik communities were designed by architects, Fournier Gersowitz, Moss, and the engineering firm, Stavibel.

These housing units are built to meet the Société d'habitation du Québec (SHQ) standards established over the years, with the Nunavik climate in mind. Close contact between Makivik and the Kativik Municipal Housing Bureau (KMHB) in the design of the houses has allowed for a standardization of materials and equipment used in the construction. This standardization allows for easier maintenance and operation of the units once they are transferred to KMHB.

The houses are well insulated with six inches of fiberglass between the studs and another inch and a half of Styrofoam behind the siding. The floors and roofs have 12 inches of insulation. To remain stable in strong northern winds, the houses are also completely covered with wood sheeting, rather than just strengthened in the corners as one would normally build for less windy areas.

As with the marine infrastructures, the objectives of Makivik's housing program is to maximize the number of Inuit employees and the number of units built, while at the same time maintaining quality construction.

The decision in 2001 to build duplexes rather than single family units is one example of cost efficiency. While it varies from community to community, depending on the amount of backfill required, the cost of building a pad to receive the houses is significant. A duplex is built on a lot of 32 by 30 metres, whereas a single family unit is normally built on a lot of approximately 22 to 25 by 30 meters.

A maximum of four or five communities are slated to receive houses in a given year. This not only helps in terms of managing the various sites, but also in terms of the cost per site. For example, if we were to build two duplexes in each of the 14 communities, versus seven duplexes in four communities, the difference in the cost per unit would be significant. The direct costs of setting up and operating a

construction camp, and flying in licensed experts such as electricians, plumbers, and engineers is basically the same whether you are building two duplexes or seven duplexes.

In 2000, a five year funding agreement was signed between the federal government, the Québec government, KRG, and Makivik, which provided for $10 million per year to build houses in Nunavik. Québec undertook to fund the deficit in operating expenses over the life of the houses (estimated at 20 years). The federal government provides $50 million for construction while the provincial government would support the operation of the units (estimated at approximately $50 million). Meanwhile, there is a renewal clause in the agreement that ends in 2004 and Makivik is negotiating this renewal with government.

In order to make full use of Nunavik's limited building season, machinery and construction materials normally are delivered to the following year's construction sites each autumn. For example, six duplex houses in Kuujjuaq got under way this past spring using materials brought up in the fall of 2002, while the materials for five other buildings arrived later in the summer when the ships were moving again. This also saves money, as it costs less to build during the warmer months because workers can perform at a fuller capacity than if they have to continually stop to warm themselves up, or to clear snow from the work site.

Makivik does all of the construction work on the Marine Infrastructure and Housing Program on a non-profit basis in order to be able to provide as many housing units, breakwaters, and wharves as possible.

There is great satisfaction in the obvious benefits of these efforts to Nunavik communities. Inuit across the region are now receiving new homes and better facilities for boat and canoe operations, as well as economic spin-offs and jobs. Being able to witness these benefits take shape within the communities is the greatest gift of all, especially from the Makivik Construction Division's point of view.

(Makivik Magazine, Fall 2003, page 9)

Sammy Kudluk

Makivik Constructs Multiplex Building for Chisasibi Inuit

Makivik Corporation had initiated a contract with Construction Chartel in late spring of 2003 to build a multipurpose structure for the Inuit of Chisasibi. This, after the leaders of the community had expressed a desire for such a structure during the last executive field trip undertaken in the winter of 2001.

The contract was signed after several revisions of what the structure should house. There was a definite need to have the building operate in some commercial capacity so that it could generate revenues to offset the operation and maintenance costs. At first, a tanning centre was considered, but was rejected by the community.

The building will have several activities associated with it. There is a fast-food restaurant, a conference room, an area for youth that is wired for computers, a wood-working shop, a sewing centre room, and an arts and crafts store. They will also have a yard protected by a chain-link fence to hold the community-owned elders vehicle, snowmobiles, canoes and outboard motors.

Richard Weetaluktuk of Chisasibi has worked with Makivik, Chartel, as well as the local Creé Band Council, to ensure the construction goes smoothly. The Creé Band Council met with Makivik representatives when required and graciously revised their community development plans to accommodate the project, including providing water and sewer services to the building site sooner than originally planned, so the construction could get underway as quickly as possible. Utaapaan Construction and Cheebee Construction received sub-contracts for this project, while four local Inuit were also hired to work on the project.

With the addition of this structure and its conference room, the Inuit community of Chisasibi can meet more often to plan for their future. The cost of the building, as per a contract signed by the Makivik executive in charge of economic development, Adamie Alaku, is set at $776,000 before taxes.

(Makivik Magazine, Winter 2003, page 45)

New Five Year Housing Agreement

The housing shortage and overcrowding challenge grows in unison with Nunavik's fast growing population, but a significant step towards getting more new social houses was taken with the recent signing of a new five year, $140 million housing agreement between Canada, Québec and Nunavik. Only 2.6 percent of homes in Nunavik are privately owned.

The region's mayors celebrated the agreement, along with leaders from Makivik, KRG, SHQ and the provincial government in Kuujjuaq this past June 27th. At the official announcement in Kuujjuaq, hosted by KRG chairman Johnny Adams, were Makivik president Pita Aatami, Québec's Minister of Municipal Affairs and Regions Nathalie Normandeau, KMHB president Maggie Emudluk, and SHQ president Pierre Cliche. Federal Minister of Indian Affairs and Northern Development Andy Scott and Québec Minister for Native Affairs Geoffrey Kelley did not make it to Kuujjuaq for the official announcement, although they each were key participants in this achievement.

Besides Makivik's ongoing political drive to see that this and other Inuit rights stemming from the JBNQA are implemented, the Corporation's Construction Division is responsible to build Nunavik's social houses. When it was Pita Aatami's turn to express his appreciation on behalf of all Inuit in Nunavik, he turned to Minister Normandeau, saying, "Thank you very much for having confidence in us and we look forward to the next five years. I also want to thank the mayors because it has been a team effort. The renewal of this agreement will certainly help to alleviate the housing shortage that the Inuit of Nunavik have unfortunately been experiencing."

Pita also explained that, although the new agreement is estimated to provide for the building of 275 new houses, the exact number would depend on the size and configuration of houses that KMHB calls for. "I know it is still a shortfall from what we really need. In some cases we have 20 people living in a three bedroom house, so this is really unacceptable and we have to figure out a way to try to get more housing up here," he added. The Makivik president also spoke highly of the Corporation's employees who have spent so much effort on this project. "I would like to thank my own staff members for working so diligently, especially construction manager Eileen Klinkig who was very instrumental in getting the government to come on board," he said.

Maggie described the dire need for more houses by stating, "We have about 150 houses in Nunavik with three families living in them and 200 houses with two families in them. This is how high our overcrowding is. So this agreement will help a lot." She also talked about the many houses that are deteriorating and need to be fixed up, which will require more funding.

During the meeting, Johnny Adams raised other related issues, mainly an error in a bylaw of the new social housing rent scale, which Pierre Cliche has since confirmed in writing that the SHQ will initiate the necessary steps to rectify, as well as the need for more houses for Kativik Regional Police officers.

Gifts were exchanged during a nice supper that evening. One of the most à propos was a soapstone carving of an igloo for David Cliche, illustrating the kind of dwellings Inuit lived in in the past, but hopefully will not have to resort to again because of the housing shortage. And the best expression of affection to Natalie Normandeau for her delivery of such good news from the government was a big kiss on the cheek from Quaqtaq Mayor Johnny Oovaut, caught by Pita Aatami's camera.

(Makivik Magazine, Summer 2005, page 50)

Transport Officials Meet in Nunavik
By Isabelle Dubois

Transport Canada Minister Jean C. Lapierre and Québec Transport Minister Julie Boulet were in Kuujjuaq at
the beginning of August to meet with Nunavik officials
and discuss various transportation topics of importance.

On August 2nd, during a press conference held at the
Kuujjuaq airport, Lapierre announced a $14,390,000 fed-
eral commitment for the construction of a new airport
terminal building and expansion of the runway apron and
parking lot, as well as other related work. The two year
project is scheduled to begin in the spring of 2006.

The Kuujjuaq airport is considered a gateway to the
North, especially to other Nunavik communities. It is an
essential link for emergency services and freight delivery.
"In addition to ensuring the safety of airport users, this investment will serve to respond to the ever increasing needs
for shipping, tourism and travel in Canada's North," said
Lapierre. Lapierre, Transport Canada officials and Makivik
and KRG leaders met in Makivik's head office boardroom. Issues such as the high cost of shipping, the need
for security at unloading docks, the lack of funding for
the operation and maintenance of marine infrastructures,
and the need for improvements to navigational safety were
discussed.

The presidents of First Air and Air Inuit brought the
imperative need for various upgrades to other Nunavik

airports to the minister's attention. Most were built over 20 years ago and are becoming inadequate as the population grows. They also discussed the needs for reliable automatic weather systems, paved runways in northern communities, and emergency generators for runway lights.

The still unsettled offshore negotiations and the need for an inquiry into the dog slaughters were also raised at the table, as Lapierre is also the minister responsible for Québec in the federal Liberal caucus.

Québec transportation issues

A meeting was held the following day, August 3rd, with Québec Minister Boulet, where many of the same issues were discussed. The assistant to Québec's minister of Transport, Michel Després, also met with officials in the KRG boardroom concerning the use of off-highway vehicles such as all terrain vehicles and snowmobiles. Boulet was informed that these vehicles are not only used for recreation, as in the south, but are mostly utilitarian modes of transport as well as for traditional hunting and gathering.

Due to the high cost of shipping and vehicle maintenance, as well as rough road conditions in the North, these off-highway vehicles are well adapted to Nunavik. As Makivik president Pita Aatami reminded the minister, "Those vehicles are used in Nunavik like cars and trucks are used down south and should be considered as such." After the discussions, Makivik and KRG submitted a brief asking that the situation of Nunavik residents be eligible for compensation in the event of injury caused by off-highway vehicles. The brief also brought up the high cost of vehicle insurance in the North, yet vehicles need to be insured for the Québec Automobile Insurance Society (SAAQ) to cover any indemnity to victims of road accidents in Nunavik.

Other issues such as the need for a SAAQ office in Nunavik and potential funding for trails were also discussed.

After hearing these concerns, Boulet promised that these issues would be addressed as much as possible with the Inuit of Nunavik's reality in mind. She also signed an agreement with KRG to extend the airfare reduction program for another year.

Besides visiting Kuujjuaq, Boulet also paid a quick visit to Kangiqsualujjuaq and had lunch with their mayor and other local leaders. She wanted to see what it was like in a smaller village than Kuujjuaq, which she has been told can be considered atypical in comparison to the smaller Nunavik communities. She saw the village's marine infrastructure and went to the local Co-op store to see the effect of high shipping costs on retail goods.

(Makivik Magazine, Fall 2005, page 18)

Kativik Senior Education Centre
Closed Until September

The Kativik Senior Education Centre in Dorval has been closed because the students have no place to stay when they were asked to leave the Travel Lodge Motel. Apparently, during the last weekend of February, a couple of students had a party that was a little too wild, and caused considerable damage to the Motel. Because of actions of a few students, all the students from the Kativik School Board who had been living at the Travel Lodge were told by the management to leave. Since there was no other place for the students to live the Senior Education Centre was closed.

In other news, the delegates at a joint meeting with various organizations in Payne Bay passed a resolution advising the school board to move its high school North as soon as possible. Generally, from the tone of things, the delegates did not seem very happy with Kativik School Board's performance to date.

The Kativik School Board is receiving criticism and suggestions to move the high school North. The Senior Education Center was closed until September after students were forced to leave the Travel Lodge Motel after a party that caused damage to the property.

(Atuaqnik, April 1979, page 9)

First Steps of the Regional Police Force

The Québec Police Force (QPF) and the Kativik Regional Government have presented the communities of Northern Québec with a proposal that will greatly increase the police services in the territory over the next 2 years.

In mid April, the presidents of all the community councils, including POV and Ivujivik, met in Fort Chimo to discuss a plan that would provide a policeman or constable with the necessary equipment in all Northern Québec communities with a population of approximately 200 or more. The plan to extend police services in Northern Québec would also involve the training of as many as 14 Inuit or local people in police operations and duties.

The proposal, which was developed by the QPF with the cooperation of the regional government must be approved by a resolution from the different community councils before it can come into effect. The regional government expects to receive the answers from the councils by the end of April, and if everything works out as planned, the hiring and training of local people will begin this May and the police equipment will be supplied this summer to all communities where it is necessary.

One of the reasons that led to the proposal to extend the police services in the territory is that under the James Bay and Northern Québec Agreement, the Kativik Regional Government is responsible for providing and establishing a regional police force for the territory North

of the 55th parallel. According to the agreement, this regional police force is to be run by the regional government
and it will take over from the QPF. Generally, it will be the
duty of the regional police force to enforce the standard
provincial and federal laws and those passed by the municipal and regional governments. Also, in the future, it may be
possible the members of the regional police force will be
assigned other special duties such as firefighting, first aid,
wildlife conservation, food inspection, and the giving of
rabies shots to the domestic dog population.

However, the Kativik Regional Government just been
set up and, at this time, it is not really ready to establish
a regional police force. In addition, there would not be
enough people from the territory that are properly trained
in police matters to fill all the positions in a regional force.

Instead of establishing a regional police force immediately, the proposal that was submitted to the communities
would see the QPF continue to provide police services in
Northern Québec for another two years. During this time
the QPF will hire and train a local people from most of the
communities and supply them with the necessary police
equipment in their settlement.

By the end of the 2 year period, the QPF will supposed
to have organized an overall police structure for Northern
Québec and helped train as many as 14 local people in
basic and advanced police techniques. At that time, if the
regional government so decides, it will be able to establish its own regional police force that will take over from
where the QPF left off.

The following is a brief description of the number of policemen and the amount of equipment each community would receive under the proposal now being considered.

Fort Chimo would be the main base for the Ungava Coast police operations and Great Whale would be the same for the Hudson Coast. There would be 3 QPF officers and 2 Inuit constables stationed in these two communities. At the beginning of the two year period, each would be equipped with a four wheel drive truck, 2 snowmobiles, 2 dune buggies, and the necessary offices. Later, the Great Whale and Fort Chimo police would be supplied with a boat. The only difference between the list of supplies is that Great Whale will get one extra truck, probably due to the fact that it will soon be connected by road with the south.

Aupaluk and Tasiujak would not have a policeman stationed in their communities and would be under the responsibility of the Fort Chimo detachment. However, if the population of these communities increases, there are plans to provide a local policeman.

Inukjuak, George River, and Payne Bay will start off with one Inuk constable each equipped with the following: one four wheel drive truck, one snowmobile, one dune buggy, and offices. Later these communities are suppose to get a boat and firefighting and basic paramedical services.

Sugluk and Wakeham will get the same as just described, but without the dune buggy, and Akulivik, Ivujivik and Koartak also get everything except for the truck.

Povungnituk will get everything mentioned above, but

because of its larger size, there will be 2 Inuit constables stationed there and their equipment will include an extra truck.

(Atuaqnik, May 1979, page 13)

Inuit Train for Police Positions

Last August twelve Inuit from Northern Québec went south to continue their training in police duties and to be officially sworn in as Special Constables.

Eventually the training and ceremonies will provide the basis for establishing a Regional Police Force for the area North of the 55th parallel. Such a regional police force would be administered by the Kativik Regional Government and would take over the duties now handled by Sureté du Québec (The Québec Police Force). In the meantime the regional government has given the Sûreté du Québec the dual responsibility of providing police services and training local people in police matters.

From August 11 to 18, a group of 12 Inuit from communities from both coasts went south for training that was provided by the Sûreté du Québec. During their first week down south they went to the headquarters of the Québec Police Force in Montréal for what is called "introduction week." At this time they were given "the usual haircut," explanations on their duties, medical exams, and they were fitted with new uniforms.

A few days later the Inuit trainees flew to Rouyn for still more instruction. It was there, on August 15th, that they were officially sworn in as Special Constables. This was done in a ceremony by Judge Jean-Charles Coutu, in the presence of some of the officers of the North West District of the Sûreté du Québec.

A few days later the new Inuit officers were invited to the ranch of the judge where they were shown a horse jumping demonstration. In addition, each of the new constables were given a chance to try a little horse riding of their own.

While in Rouyn-Noranda, the twelve Inuit followed courses in human behaviour, policeman tactics, a preliminary course in crime scene, court roll, photography and camera use, firearms registration, the role of the crime scene, a preliminary course in protecting the scene of a crime, and, at last, firearms manipulation. Apparently it was the first time the Sûreté du Québec (The Québec Police Force) gave these courses in English. One the police officials said all of these courses went well, "with the great cooperation of the Inuit police officers."

According to the Sûreté du Québec, the Inuit Special Constables will be returning in the future for more courses in administration and mecanical prevention.

The material for this article were provided by the Sûrete du Québec.

(Atuaqnik, November 1979, page 21)

Jobs For Inuit At Caniapiscau Project
By M. McGoldrick

According to officials with the James Bay Energy Corporation, there are possible employment opportunities for the Inuit at the Caniapiscau construction site, which is part of the James Bay hydroelectric project.

During a recent tour of the site by a group of Kuujjuaq residents, a manpower official from the site explained to representatives of the Kativik Regional Government, the Makivik Corporation, and *Atuaqnik* newspaper that it was possible for Inuit to find work at the Caniapiscau construction site. He also explained that the Agreement gives some preference to native people who are seeking work on the project.

Individuals or groups can apply for jobs at the site. The work generally became available in early spring and lasts throughout the summer until late fall. The person who applies may have to wait anywhere from a few weeks to a few months before there is a job opening.

Most of the workers on the site live in large staff houses that have many modem conveniences such as flushing toilets, telephones, and television. There are two workers per bedroom, and there are 24 workers per staff house.

The jobs range from office work to heavy construction work. Depending on the job one gets, the pay is anywhere from $8 to $12 an hour. After 50 hours of work a week, you get time and a half, and after 60 hours, it becomes double time. Considering that no one on the site works less than 60 hours a week, and some hardy individuals work as much as 84 hours a week, there is a lot of money being paid out in salaries. Furthermore, food and lodging is free for those who work on the site.

If anyone is interested in applying to work at the Caniapiscau, they should contact Charlie Saviardjuk, the Manpower Councillor at the Kativik Regional Government.

(Atuaqnik, November 1979, page 24)

Sammy Kudluk

Kigiak Builders

A lot of people were interested in finding out more about Kigiak builders. In Great Whale they asked about possible jobs and training with Kigiak, including whether or not it is necessary to be able to speak English to get such jobs with the construction company. Mr. Watt answered that anyone could approach Kigiak if they want to work for the company. He also explained that people could chose the type of work they would like to receive training in, such as electrical, carpentry, plumbing or mechanics. In Akulivik it was explained that there are twenty-one Inuit working for Kigiak.

Generally, Charlie Watt described the equipment Kigiak now has and how it will operate. He said that it had a cement factory and a large rock crusher. At the moment the rock crusher is being used to build up a five year supply of crushed rock for Chimo and then it will be transported to the other settlements to ensure that all communities will get enough gravel.

In Inukjuak the people who attended the meeting suggested that it would be an improvement if it would be possible for Kigiak to take over MTPA.

(Atuaqnik, December 1979, page 12)

The Jobs & Training You Want At Kigiak
By Willie Adams

According to Kigiak General Manager, Dennis Jutras, there will be many positions and training opportunities for any Inuk who is interested in working in the construction business.

"I don't want to hire local people as labourers," said Mr. Jutras, adding that, "I want them to try to choose a trade so that it will be a lot easier for us. I like to know in advance, if we hire someone, we will be training them in something they like."

At the moment, Kigiak is establishing itself and is building its service centre in Kuujjuaq. However, they plan to be ready to provide some services in the communities this coming summer or maybe even this spring.

"Right now we're getting the construction company started. We have to build the service centre which will service all the communities with materials, not only Kuujjuaq, we want to serve all the communities. But the service centre has to be done first."

Kigiak plans to make a list of the available manpower in the communities. They will rely on this to hire construction crews right on site rather than have their own crews travel all over the place.

Mr. Jutras stressed that one of the main goals of Kigiak was to rely on local or northern resource as much as possible, and to import as little as possible from the south. He

said that this kind of thinking will apply to everything, including construction materials, labour and skilled tradesmen. For example Kigiak's rock crusher and concrete plant will mean they will be able to use more local materials instead of always importing expensive building supplies from the south. And of course, much of Kigiak's labour needs will be hired in the communities. In addition, by providing good training opportunities this will mean that Northerners will also fill the positions where skilled tradesmen are needed. Mr. Jutras added that this policy to rely on northern resource will save some money that would otherwise have gone toward transportation and travel expenses.

He explained this situation by saying, "at the moment everything is brought from Montréal or Toronto, but we want to be self sufficient."

In order to help reach their goal of self sufficiency Kigiak will have a carpentry, mechanical, machine and electrical shops so they won't have to depend so much on the south.

Mr. Jutras stated that Kigiak would also like to have people from outside of Kuujjuaq working for them. He said people who are interested in this should write to him.

At the moment, Kigiak is keeping busy with construction of its service centre and Makivik staff house which should be completed in a month and half. But they are also negotiating a contract with the Kativik School Board, which if successful, would see Kigiak build a duplex in Aupaluk as part of the school's staff housing. Mr. Jutras says that if they get it, they will probably send in one or two of their regular crew and hire the labour from Aupaluk. Kigiak is also interested in building some of the houses that the Québec Housing Corporation (QHC) plans to bring up this year. But there is nothing definite because the QHC is not sure of what kind of housing design it will bring up. Nothing concrete came out of a meeting between them and Kigiak.

Mr. Jutras explained to date Makivik has spent up to $3 million on setting up Kigiak. He added that Makivik could start receiving some revenues from the construction company in 3 years, and that the Kigiak Maintenance Division could help in accomplishing this.

People interested in working or if they want more information about Kigiak they should write to them at: P.O. Box 104 Kuujjuaq (Ft. Chimo) Quebec.

(Atuaqnik, February 1980, page 15)

Grade 11 in Oil Communities a Priority for K.S.B.
Willie Adams

The High School in Dorval for Inuit Students of Northern Québec will probably not be opening for quite some time, explained Adamie Inukpuk, the President of the Kativik School Board (KSB).

In a telephone interview with *Atuaqnik*, Mr. Inukpuk said he was not really sure when the high school will open again, explaining that the school board has since given priority to making sure that students can complete up to grade 11 in their own communities. He also said the school in Dorval will not reopen until they find out if the people in Northern Québec are in favour of continuing to have a high school in the south for Inuit students.

Although the President of the school board spoke about not knowing exactly when the Dorval High School would reopen, one also gets the impression that it is very possible that it may never reopen again. There was a plan to reopen the troubled high school in September, 1979, but this never came about for the reasons stated by Mr. Adamie Inukpuk. The school suddenly closed almost a year ago when trouble by a few students caused all students to be kicked out of the place where they were being lodged.

At the moment, the Kativik School Board says they are concentrating on their plans to enable students to complete up to grade 11 without having to leave their communities. However, Mr. Inukpuk said that they were having some problems in the hiring of teachers for the project. There is also the problem of a shortage of houses for these teachers in the communities. As a result, a few communities now have up to grade 11 at the moment

"We have mentioned building a High School in Northern Québec, but we can't say it will be right away," said Mr. Inukpuk. At the last meeting of the commissioners, this subject was brought up, but it is not known when or if such a high school will be built in Northern Québec, and the question has yet to be resolved. However, Adamie Inukpuk continued to explain that the matter will probably be discussed at a meeting of the different organizations to be held in Montréal.

In another project, the KSB wanted to use a TV system as a teaching aid in the schools. This project was supposed to be in collaboration with Taqramiut Nipingat Inc. (TNI), but there have been some financial problems. Mr. Inukpuk said he didn't know what the outcome of the project will be.

In other news concerning the KSB, the School Board has their own flag design. The flag is blue and white with a picture of their crest on it, and the schools in all the communities will receive one. Mr. Inukpuk said that they have a T-shirt with their design, but that it is not ready yet.

(Atuaqnik, January 1980, page 5)

Makivik Steps up Training Activities

Makivik's Training Service has developed an enhanced training program for 1987-1988, and a special budget request to the Executive Committee has been approved for the implementation of a complete plan of action. Makivik is contributing $40,000 to this effort.

This plan helps develop Makivik's policy of providing proper training for Inuit staff and other personnel, and will help continue the relocation of Makivik's activities to Nunavik. Makivik can then plan the relocation of more positions to the North.

The plan for 1987-1988 will include some long term activities. For example, in cooperation with the Adult Ed. Services of KSB, part-time courses will be offered both for Makivik employees and all interested northerners. Specific training activities will be developed for those interested in computers, accounting, secretarial skills, translation, and syllabic typing. The Training Service also plans to offer management workshops and seminars.

Makivik always aims to integrate new Inuit staff into its employment structure. This means job creation, and providing the right kind of instruction for new trainees. The Training Service is working on programs for a receptionist, cartographer, journalist, and secretaries.

It is well known that Inuit young people have an especially difficult time finding work in the North. In addition to slowing down economic development, lack of jobs for young people causes some serious social problems in our communities. This is shown by the fact that the great majority of young people from 15 to 30 years old are inactive.

In response to this need, the Training Officer has organized a pilot project for students. The project will provide part-time jobs for students in areas that compliment their school education. It is hoped that apprenticeship experience will promote higher scholarship among our CEGEP and graduating secondary school students.

Current Makivik employees will also benefit from training activities that may make them eligible for promotions. For example, secretaries could learn about administration or office management.

Finally, several specific job development projects are already underway, such as the training of crewmen for SEAKU Fisheries. Other Makivik subsidiaries will be able to integrate new Inuit employees, and students will find more summer job projects available to them. The eventual caribou commercialization project will also be served by the Training Service's long term planning.

(Makivik News, November 1987, page 19)

Youth Training: A New Beginning
By Teddy Shulman

Makivik's Youth Agent Training Project will be ending in September 1995. This project started two years ago with three local community Youth Agents whose training and activities were co-ordinated by Sarah Airo and her trainer Bertran Michaud.

Two major goals of the program were sensitization to social issues and enhancing awareness of the political process. A few accomplishments towards these goals can be seen with Kuujjuaq hosting the First International Youth meeting last November, our work with local Youth Committees, the development of their "Committee Working Guide" and the incorporation of the newly created Nunavik Youth Association.

Our original intention was to hand over the coordination of the Youth Agent training to KRG's Recreation Department, and this will happen next September.

In the next five months, local Youth Agents will be organizing at least three new summer camps. Plans are well underway for our third KRG funded "Stay In School" Science Camp at Abloviaq Fjord to introduce 36 new participants of the Ungava Coast to science and technology. We are also excited about Salluit's upcoming concert with Susan Aglukark.

Meetings with KSB and KRG are planned for April to coordinate how each organization can best utilize their resources to most effectively support Nunavik's youth. Though Makivik's Youth Agent Training Project is ending, our dedication and commitment to the youth remains firm.

Sarah Airo will assume the position of Makivik's Youth Political Liaison. She will represent Nunavik's youth at regional, national and international meetings. Part of her responsibility will be to ensure the youth file Makivik developed over the last five years will be integrated into the KRG/KSB program starting up again in September.

(Makivik News, Spring 1995, page 55)

Training to Fish the Offshore Shrimp
By Stephen Hendrie

The factory freezer trawlers operating the Seaku, Un-aaq, and Qikiqtaaluk shrimp licenses require all seamen to possess certain training in order to be on board. In addition to this, to attain a position that will elevate a fisherman from a worker on deck to a position inside the Captain's cabin, even more training is required.

The job of training Inuit fishermen has been the task of Unaaq Fisheries, jointly owned by Seaku Fisheries and Qikiqtaaluk Corporation. In turn, Unaaq has mandated the Kativik School Board (KSB) to develop training programs for Inuit in Nunavik. This. KSB has done over the past 10 years, as long as Seaku Fisheries has existed.

Jackie Koneak, Makivik's former Second Vice-President overseeing the work of Seaku Fisheries, is proud of the fact that over 100 Inuit from Nunavik have been employed over the years for Seaku Fisheries on board the vessels. He says. "We are getting some officers now. Inuit have gone through all the categories, from deckhand, all the way up to second mate."

At KSB, this was borne out by Steven Wanamaker, who has worked on developing training courses for the past ten years. KSB is mandated through the James Bay Agreement, as the school board for the Nunavik region. KSB's Adult Education–Vocational Training Department has the mandate to develop the training. Wanamaker has been involved in creating training programs and sending prospective Inuit fishermen to courses in Port Hawksbury, and Pictou, in Nova Scotia; St. Romuald, and Gaspé, Québec; St. John's Newfoundland, and also in Nunavik.

A basic course given to prospective Inuit fishermen is the 30 hour Marine Emergency Duties Course (MED-1). The MED-1 certification is required by the Canadian coast guard to be able to board the ship.

While flying Inuit to points south has been commonplace in the past, the more recent trend is to find a southern based instructor, and bring the instructor, and the required gear to Nunavik to give the training. This was the case in February when a MED-1 course was given at the Adult Education Center in Kuujjuaraapik. Ten Inuit took part in the two week course. An instructor from the Marine Institute in St. John's, Newfoundland, Rob Gibbins, was flown in to give the course.

The MED-1 course covers some basic first aid instruction, firefighting, and emergency ship evacuation. In Kuujjuaraapik, the students donned firefighting gear and extinguished fires during part of the course. Wanamaker says abandoning ship is required in extreme cases because of dangerous weather conditions, a fire on board, or if there is too much ice build-up on the exterior of the ship.

To simulate the abandon ship drill in Kuujjuaraapik, the group needed some open water. In Kuujjuaraapik, in February, with temperatures hovering at -20° celsius most of the time, there was no open water. They thought of cutting a hole in one of the nearby lakes, but the lakes were frozen

to the bottom. So, with the help of municipal workers, a 15x30 foot pool made of snow banks was created using snow plows. The inside banks were sprayed with water to create a hard ice surface. On the day of the exercise, the pool was filled with water. It was a windy, blustery day, with some precipitation—perfect weather for an abandon ship simulation!

Bright red survival suits covered almost every inch of their bodies, except their faces. Once the students had put them on, they walked outside of the Adult Education building to the place where the pool had been built. It was one of the more unusual sights seen in Kuujjuaraapik for quite some time—10 men dressed in bright red neoprene suits from head to toe carrying a large white bubble. The bubble contained an inflatable raft.

Many people visited the site where the simulation took place over the lunch hour. They observed the students swimming in formation in the suits. This is done to reduce panic, and to create a larger shape in the water, likely to be spotted by search and rescue planes or helicopters. Except for one person, whose suit had torn, all the students were able to withstand an afternoon dip in the open water, under the driving snow and frigid February temperatures in Kuujjuaraapik.

Of the 10 students taking the course, Wanamaker says five were soon bound for a journey on board the Aqviq, while the remaining five would be called in a few months.

While many Inuit have experienced life on board the offshore trawlers as deckhands, fewer have made it up the ranks into the Captain's cabin as a third or second mate. A Fishing Master Class Four license is required to attain these positions, as well as accumulating at least 365 days of sea duty.

At the Marine Institute in St. John's, Newfoundland, nine Inuit fishermen embarked on the nine week training course which ends April 4th. Wanamaker says the course requires good math skills. Second and third mates are involved with navigating the ship, which means working with plenty of charts, radar, and radio equipment. The students must pass an exam for the Canadian Coast Guard in order to obtain their Fishing Master Class 4 License.

Peter Keenainak, Manager at Unaaq Fisheries, and Stephen Wanamaker at KSB visited the students in St. John's while they were taking the course to ensure that they were managing with the heavy course load. Reached on March 14th, with three weeks left in the course, Wanamaker noted that the course was going fine, that some of the fishermen were encountering difficulties with their math, but that the work was progressing well.

The successful students who pass the course will have other hurdles to overcome. Positions in the Captain's cabin are highly sought after, not only by the growing number of Inuit fishermen, but also by the many seamen in Newfoundland.

In an Unaaq Fisheries newsletter, Kinguksiut. an article by Peter Keenainak chronicles some fascinating statistics about the numbers of Inuit fishermen trained over the years. For example, "Since 1991, Unaaq has organized 17 different courses ranging from pre-sea to Fishing Master IV with a total of 189 individuals participating." Inuit from Nunavik, and Nunavut are working on three ships which fish the licenses held by Seaku, Unaaq, and Qikiqtaaluk. The ships are the Aqviq, Kinguk, Atlantic Enterprise, and Arctic Prawns. The average number of sea-days completed by the 48 active fishermen as of October 1995 was 542. Jamie Etok is listed as having worked 1613 sea-days on the Aqviq.

Developing a trained workforce has taken years to accomplish. It is an ongoing task. Word-of-mouth is now helping attract more Inuit to the industry. It is well known that the work is tough, but the life is interesting, and the pay can be quite handsome when the shrimp are plentiful.

There are new horizons to be explored in the fishing ventures. The experience gained over the years by Seaku and Unaaq has become valuable. It is now being shared with aboriginal peoples in other underdeveloped countries. Recent travels made by Makivik Treasurer Pita Aatami to visit the Mesquito Indians in Nicaragua, and Corporate Secretary Sheila Watt-Cloutier to Fiji, the Solomon Islands, Papua New Guinea, and Vanuatu, are testaments to this work. This will be the subject of a further installment in this series of articles on Makivik's fisheries activities. So, as they say in pidgin English, in Fiji, "Yu ken kam bak an reed nex tim, tasol."

(Makivik News, Spring 1996, page 16)

Montréal Career Assistance
By Carolyn Stone

Inuit living in Montréal or the surrounding areas are eligible for funds allocated for training and employment measures through the Aboriginal Workforce Association of Montréal (AWAM). The Association is a non-profit organization which caters to the Urban Aboriginal Community, serving those of Inuit, First Nations and Métis ancestry who have lived in the area for more than three months.

AWAM was incorporated in 1996 as a Community Development Organization to provide assistance to individuals who lack certain training or opportunities to secure full time permanent employment in a field of their interest. While the Association is not in the business of getting jobs for native people, they assist to develop talents, reach goals and support individuals committed to their chosen career.

In order to reach all necessary training needs, AWAM works under the four measures of support and guidance, training and professional development, workforce stabilization, and employability.

Over the past summer, AWAM funded approximately 20 native students for summer positions. Some of the organizations which took part were Taqramiut Nipingat Inc., the Kativik School Board, Aboriginal Women of Montréal, Concordia University, and McGill University.

Currently, AWAM is looking to expand into the realm of economic development. AWAM provides employment services to the Aboriginal urban population offered through Aboriginal Employment Services located at the Native Friendship Centre of Montréal. They have also assisted in the development of a Native Craft Store in Old Montréal. Anyone living in the city who thinks they may benefit from AWAM services is encouraged to call.

(Makivik Magazine, Fall 1998, page 61)

Sammy Kudluk

Headstart in Ottawa

Makivik Magazine was in Ottawa for the third National Aboriginal Headstart Training Workshop, September 13–15, 1998, called "Strengthening Children and Families." While Aboriginal communities from across Canada were represented there, the Inuit from the various northern regions evidently had more in common with one another than with other First Nations groups. Lisa Epoo, Eva Kasudluak, and Louisa Whiteley-Tukkiapik were also there from Nunavik.

The Government of Canada established Aboriginal Headstart in 1995 "to help enhance child development and school readiness of Indian, Métis, and Inuit children living in urban centres and large northern communities."

Headstart is a federally funded program, free to the parents. The initiative responds to the recommendation of the Royal Commission on Aboriginal Peoples and the need to ensure the healthy development of all Aboriginal children. Parents and grandparents are graciously urged to participate. It is for children from infants to five year olds, and includes components of culture and language, education, health promotion, nutrition, social support programs, and parental involvement

Children are seen as the nation's most valuable resource. The program is based on creativity and pride flowing from the knowledge of their traditional beliefs, within an holistic and safe environment.

Headstart offers practically the same services as regular daycare. However, unlike the daycare program which usually runs from 9 a.m. to 5 p.m., Headstart children go for half-days. In certain cases, the child will be going to the Headstart section and his mother finds a job, so he will then go into the full-time daycare.

Headstart is designed for children who do not necessarily need to be in daycare because their parents or other caregivers are unavailable to look after them, but who need further socialization and stimulation to give them a "head start" in child development. It helps to prepare the children for school. As Lisa Epoo, Director of the Tasiurvik Childcare Centre in Inukjuak explains, in the beginning they met with kindergarten teachers to find out where they could help the children most. Now, when these kids go to kindergarten, they already know the basics such as their syllables, how to use scissors, to colour, and to write their names. They have also already become acquainted with the classroom setting.

Unlike regular daycare programs which are available throughout the year, the Headstart program does not run in the summer. They are generally open during the school year.

Health Canada says the Headstart Program is "not just a matter of Aboriginal Peoples running our own schools, but Aboriginals setting good examples for Canada and for the world."

Pierre Pettigrew, Minister of Human Resources Canada, was a keynote speaker during a lunch there. Among the points he touched on during his speech, he explained that social investments in society are good for economic development. "We should not be talking about social costs as expenses, but rather as investments," he told the audience.

Ethel Blondin-Andrew, Secretary of State (Children and Youth) with Human Resources, also made a presentation during a banquet at the Ottawa Native Friendship Centre to conclude the seminars. She emphasized the benefits of interaction between elders and children, and of preserving Aboriginal languages.

She also noted that, "As a single mother, I could have used the Headstart program if it was available then."

"Self esteem and a sense of identity is one of the greatest gifts you can give a child. Secure children will become secure adults who will hold their own in cross-cultural (and other) situations," she said, "An insecure child will become an insecure adult."

She also sees education as a route out of poverty. While it is privilege in some other countries, it is a right for all Canadians. "It used to be that a parent would just send their children off to school to do whatever, and that was it. Now parents are more involved," she stated.

(Makivik Magazine, Summer 1999, page 17)

Most Post-Secondary Graduates Ever

More post-secondary students graduated from programs of study in 1999 than in any previous year. Larry Watt, Executive Assistant/Co-Department Head for the Makivik president's office congratulated all the graduates, stating:"Makivik Corporation is extremely grateful for the immense effort shown by the post-secondary graduates of Nunavik. Post-secondary education in both the academic and vocational fields is increasingly important in our diverse and ever changing modern society. The graduates, who possess knowledge of Nunavik's culture, language and society have grasped a significant potential for contributing to the betterment of lives and for obtaining skills that will lead to an active and visionary approach in Nunavik's organizations. The corporation, which is continuing its efforts in moving jobs to Nunavik, would like to state its optimistic view that it will be able to hire more educated personnel from within its region." His message was provided to the *Makivik Magazine* in a memorandum. Larry Watt graduated from Ianimmarik School in 1988, Dawson College in 1993, and received a BA in Political Science from Concordia University in 1996.

Graduating from John Abbott College were Sarollie Inukpuk (Inukjuak, Social Science), Christina Mesher (Kuujjuaq/Social Science), Tommy Moorehouse (Inukjuak/Social Science), Aloupa Taqulik (Kangirsuk/Social Science), Raymond Meeko (Kuujjuaraapik/Language and Literature), and Roxanne Gordon (Kuujjuaq/Police Technology). Vicky Okpik (Quaqtaq/Fashion Design) graduated from Lasalle College. Dave Chalmers (Kuujjuaq/Construction Electricity) graduated from Centre Formation Professionelle de Lachine.

There were also two "firsts" among the graduates. Martha Putugu of Puvirnituq graduated from St-Hyacinthe CEGEP, becoming the first Inuk to obtain a nursing degree in French. Also, Betsy Annahatak of Kangirsuk also became the first Inuk from Nunavik to obtain a Master's degree, graduating from McGill University in the field of Education.

In addition, there were nine graduates from McGill's Northern Community Social Workers certificate program.

(Makivik Magazine, Summer 1999, page 69)